RIVER RAFTING

By Cecil Kuhne

WORLD

World Publications, Inc.
Mountain View, California

Recommended Reading:
River World Magazine, Box 366,
Mountain View, CA 94042; $6.50/year
Write for a free catalog of publications.

Library of Congress Cataloging in Publication Data
Kuhne, Cecil, 1952-
    River rafting.

    Includes index.
    1. Rafting (Sports) I. Title.
GV780.K83   797   78-64389
ISBN 0-89037-154-7

Poem

*Have you gazed on naked grandeur where there's nothing else
to gaze on,*
Set pieces and drop-curtain scenes galore,
*Big mountains heaved to heaven, which the blinding sunsets
blazon,*
Black canyons where the rapids rip and roar?
*Have you swept the visioned valley with the green stream
streaking through it,*
Searched the vastness for a something you have lost?
*Have you strung your soul to silence? Then for God's sake go
and do it;*
Hear the challenge, learn the lesson, pay the cost.

Robert W. Service

Contents

Introduction:

River Rafting as a Sport

An inflatable raft drifts effortlessly down the river, dwarfed by canyons or mountains rising from the river's edge. Soon the rumbling sound of distant water slapping over rocks intensifies until the rapids are in sight. The raft is lined into the proper position at the head of the rapids and then glides down a smooth trough and into a mass of boiling water.

The force of the rapids engulfs the raft as it flexes through the waves. For a moment the raft hangs suspended, rocking from side to side as the churning water passes underneath. The river eventually subsides, leaving the raft half full of water and its passengers drenched.

River rafting has now come into its own, but the transition has been long and gradual. During the development of America, rapids were forces to be feared and avoided. Two factors, however, made river running a safe proposition. The techniques for running rapids were greatly refined, and much of the credit can be attributed to Nathaniel Galloway. Galloway invented the art of running rapids with the stern of the boat downstream, a method allowing a clear and easy view of the obstacles ahead.

The quality of river boats also improved. Wooden dories and cataract boats were first used, and then the surplus inflatable rafts of World War II hit the scene and were used successfully throughout the rivers of the West during the 1940s and 1950s.

The sport of rafting grew rapidly, especially in the last decade. This is not surprising because rafting offers a variety of unique experiences and perspectives not available from the shore. As the raft floats downstream, it scarcely interrupts the natural flow of the river, leaving the environment virtually unaffected.

The great demand for rafts led to advancements in materials, design, and manufacturing techniques of rafts and related rafting and camping equipment. The knowledge of river running techniques also spread. This improved equipment and widespread knowledge has contributed both to the increased safety and popularity of river rafting.

Running a raft through rapids is a skill developed by experience, and the satisfaction is great to those who do it well. A sense of style and integrity in negotiating the rapids with clean, crisp strokes is needed. River runners do not need the best possible equipment, but using good equipment and developing the skill to use that equipment will eliminate most of the danger.

Rafting, like most other pursuits, is best when kept simple. The improvement in new equipment also brings with it a rash of unnecessary gadgets. But the real beauty of rafting is found in its simplicity—riding on a mass of air surrounded by a flexible rubber form.

The thrill of river rafting, too, is not confined to the single boater who handles the oars. Paddle trips provide for even more participation in controlling the raft. And everyone can join in planning, loading equipment, rigging the raft, reading rapids, and establishing camp at the day's end. In addition to the thrill of whitewater, there are also opportunities for activities such as hiking, photography, and wildlife observation.

The camaraderie of those on a river trip is especially memorable. Spending complete days together in unfamiliar surroundings and new adventures has a way of drawing people close together. People who share this unique experience will repeat stories of the trip years later.

1

The Raft

Inflatable rafts are well suited for use as river boats. Although somewhat sluggish on flat water, the raft's flexible form is a distinct advantage in whitewater. It allows the raft to flow with the river and absorb the impact of rapids and boulders. Strong materials and multiple chambers render a river raft difficult to tear and practically impossible to sink. Designed with an upturned bow and stern, the raft takes on less water and rides the rapids more gracefully than other craft. Easily portable, the raft requires a minimum of upkeep and attention.

The inflatable raft actually received its wide acceptance as a river craft after large numbers of surplus rafts became available following World War II. Both the 7-man and 10-man assault rafts, as well as the bridge pontoons, were used with great success on rivers of the West. These big black rafts were very tough, although a bit bulky by today's standards.

The 7-man and 10-man surplus rafts are still used by both commercial and private parties, but they are now practically impossible to locate in surplus stores. Current military regulations require that used rafts be shredded, despite their condition, for fear that subsequent sale to civilians will result in lawsuits if injuries occur during use.

When these rafts became scarce, outfitters needing rafts turned to manufacturers for new models. The first raft designed specifically for river running was the Green River model designed by Del Mosser and manufactured by Rubber Fabricators. This model filled the needs of the outfitter who required a raft with a larger payload than the 10-man but smaller than surplus pontoon boats. Rubber Fabricators later expanded their line to include other fine rafts, including the Yampa, Salmon, and Snake models.

A number of raft models are now commercially manufactured in this country and abroad. These new rafts vary widely in size, extending from the 6-foot dinghy to the 37-foot Colorado River model, but rafts in the 12- to 16-foot range offer the best compromise of stability and maneuverability. Since these rafts displace only a couple inches of water, they can be floated down small rivers with a low volume of water. With proper rafting equipment and experience, they are capable of running the largest rapids. These rafts also have sufficient capacity for passengers and gear. The 7-man (12 feet long and 6½ feet wide) will accommodate 2 or 3 persons and their gear, while the 10-man (15 feet long and 7½ feet wide) has a capacity for 4 to 6 persons with gear.

Advancements in materials, design, and manufacturing techniques have contributed to the increased safety of the raft. Natural rubber was replaced long ago by neoprene, which was later replaced by DuPont Hypalon. Hypalon coatings and nylon fabrics are now widely used due to their strength and light weight. The newest fabrics on the market are Dacron polyester and DuPont Kevlar, and the most recent developments in coatings have been polyvinyl chloride (PVC) and polyurethane. Sophisticated design features allow for a raft which is more eye appealing and functional, allowing greater maneuverability and less bailing. Manufacturing techniques have also improved to ensure the strength of the raft's seams.

The number of raft manufacturers and distributors has increased likewise. Avon and Campways are two of the most widely known companies who distribute river rafts in this country. Avon rafts are manufactured in England and Campways in Japan. Rubber Fabricators, a division of B.F. Goodrich, manufactured excellent rafts for many years, but they are no longer in operation; these same models, however, are now manufactured by Rubber Crafters of West Virginia. Another American manufacturer, Mountain State Inflatables, also produces a fine line of rafts made of neoprene-coated nylon. Zodiac is a well-established French company offering several models designed for river running. A more recent entry into the market is Rogue Inflatables, which imports a number of models from Japan. Rafts constructed of the new fabrics and thermoplastic coatings (Dacron polyester/polyvinyl chloride and DuPont Kevlar/urethane) are now manufactured in the United States by Maravia Corporation.

Other less expensive rafts are available, but quality varies widely. Some of the better models of these rafts are imported from Taiwan and Japan by UDISCO and World Famous, while Northwest River Supplies distributes an excellent line of inexpensive rafts designed specifically for river running.

These inexpensive rafts maintain a definite place in the sport, because they allow access to rivers by those who do not wish to invest in the more expensive models. They are especially suitable for slower and less rocky rivers, but care should be taken not to overload them. The primary problem with the inexpensive rafts has been the thin floors that tear easily, but this can be improved somewhat by applying additional layers of neoprene/Hypalon coating, or gluing sheets of additional material, to heavily abraded areas, such as the bottom of the raft.

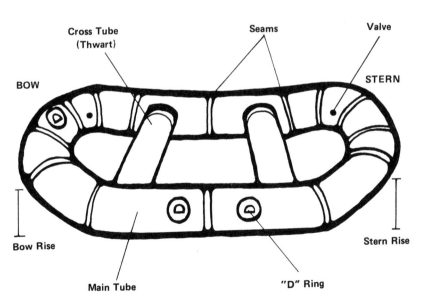

Figure 1   Features of the Raft

Raft Design

Rafts differ from one another in more than length and width. How a raft handles on the river, too, is largely dependent upon its design. The designs of rafts vary in many respects, most notably how much the bow and stern are upturned, whether the bow and stern sections are built with a sweeping curve or with compound (multiple) segments, and the diameter of the buoyancy tubes. Design, moreover, consists of more than a blueprint of the raft, for the materials and manufacturing procedures may greatly affect a particular design.

The actual design adopted may depend upon several factors —the type of river, the method of control and propulsion (oars, paddles, or motor), the number of passengers, and the length of trips. A common denominator of design does not exist. Some rafters prefer elevated bow and stern sections to assist the raft in rising over water hazards, while others prefer low bow configurations to aid the raft in driving through water obstacles. The amount of bow and stern rise varies among models, but generally, the lift will not exceed 16 inches for a 24-inch diameter tube and 14 inches for smaller tubes.

Curvature of the bow and stern is determined principally by eye appeal and the manufacturing techniques used. To obtain a sweeping, uninterrupted curve, it is necessary to cut the fabric in a banana-like fashion. While this design achieves a certain amount of eye appeal, it is a manufacturing problem in that the full width of the fabric cannot be used, thus generating a significant amount of waste. Squares of blunt-nosed shapes are derived from military crafts designed during World War II and do not represent any specific design influence based on whitewater experience.

The design of the raft may also be affected by the rigidity or flexibility of the boat. Rigidity provides greater maneuverability, assists the raft in driving through or over rapids, and provides a more graceful movement because it does not allow a "porpoising" motion. This rigidity also helps to prevent a raft, when upset, from wrapping around a boulder and becoming filled with water. Some boaters, however, prefer a looser, flexible construction which allows the raft to bend and fold as it encounters large rapids.

Rigidity, in turn, is dependent upon a number of factors, including the length of the fabric fiber, the shape of the bow and stern sections, and the manner in which the raft is manufactured. The fabrics with minimal stretch under stress and rafts with a minimum number of seams (allowing fewer points at which the fabric can bend) result in rafts that are significantly more rigid. A manufacturing trend that positions the fabric thread into the circumference of the buoyancy tube, as opposed to the horizontal line of the raft, also provides greater rigidity and strength.

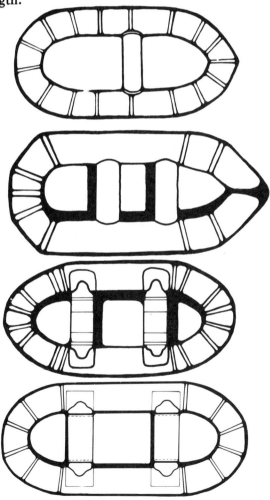

Figure 2   Types of Raft Design
Note the number and shape of segments.

Materials

Rafts are manufactured from a coated fabric, consisting of a base fabric with a protective coating bonded to it. The base fabric is usually nylon, Dacron polyester, or DuPont Kevlar, and coated usually with neoprene, Hypalon, polyvinyl chloride (PVC), or polyurethane. Generally speaking, the base fabric provides the material's strength and resistance to tearing, while the coating provides air tightness, abrasion resistance, and material longevity.

Raft manufacturers purchase these coated fabrics from suppliers who specialize in coating fabrics. These coated fabrics are manufactured according to specifications defining the strength and weight of the fabric, the type and weight of the coating compound, and the appropriate quality control tests.

Most of the nylon/neoprene rafts currently manufactured are an offshoot of World War II technology. These materials have proven themselves for many years, and a number of pontoons which were manufactured in the 1940s and 1950s are still operating in the Grand Canyon. Neoprene remained the standard coating of high quality rafts until its recent displacement by the more expensive Hypalon, offering superior resistance to abrasion and deterioration.

Significant breakthroughs in the technology of fibers and coatings used in the construction of heavy-duty inflatable boats have also occurred. These new fabrics include Dacron polyester, DuPont Kevlar, and the new plastic-style coatings such as polyvinyl chloride (PVC) and polyurethane. Although expensive, these materials offer several advantages, including light weight, reduced fiber elongation characteristics, higher tear and tensile strength, and superior resistance to abrasion and ultra violet rays.

Manufacturing Procedures

In an age of mass production, it is comforting to know that some products hold to traditional standards and are still fashioned with the care and craftsmanship of the distant past. An inflatable raft is one of those products, because a well-made raft is a meticulously engineered and personally tooled product.

Coated fabrics used in the manufacture of rafts may be purchased either in *uncured* or *cured* states. If the raft is to be manufactured according to the vulcanization process, the fabric must be of the "raw" or uncured condition. Cured materials, on the other hand, are required for rafts manufactured by an "air cured" or "cold cured" process. These cured fabrics are vulcanized by the supplier, who wraps the fabric tightly on a large steel drum and subjects it to heat and pressure in an autoclave.

Whether the rafts are vulcanized or cold cured, the same basic assembly procedures are followed. The material is unrolled on a cutting table, then doubled up, with the number of layers determined by the thickness of the material and the number of rafts to be manufactured. A pattern is placed on top of the material. All plies are cut at once with a reciprocating or rotary blade knife. The cut pieces are marked to identify their location on the raft. These pieces are then spread out on tables and glued around the edges where the material is to be lapped. Generally, two or three coats of adhesive are applied. When dry, it is dusted with zinc stearate or starch to prevent pieces from sticking together and facilitate handling.

The subsections of the raft, the bow, stern, side tubes, cross tubes, floor, and bulkheads, are the first to be assembled. The subsections are then connected together by "joiners." Joining two parts together consists of aligning, marking the seam width, activating the adhesive with a suitable solvent, and fastening the two pieces together. This sounds easy and looks simple when performed by an experienced joiner, but it is actually very difficult, because the edges of the bow and stern contain compound curves that require great skill to assemble.

The bow and stern sections are joined to the side tubes and the final peripheral seam is closed, completing the outside tubes or "rails." The cross tubes are then joined to the rails in much the same manner. After allowing the adhesive to dry, the raft is inflated to a low pressure and the floor is attached. Various patches, such as those containing "D" rings, are also attached.

CURING AND VULCANIZATION

If the raft is of cold cure construction, it is now complete except for the three to seven days necessary for the adhesive to cure. In cold cure construction the adhesive must be supplemented with an accelerator that chemically cures at room temperature and gains virtually full strength after seven days, depending upon the temperature, humidity, type of adhesive, and amount of accelerator used.

If the raft is of vulcanized construction, no accelerator is added to the adhesive, so the adhesive must now be vulcanized by a steam pressure autoclave (doctors use a small version to sterilize their instruments). The autoclave used for vulcanizing rafts consists of a large steel tank with a door on one end; it may measure up to 16 feet in diameter and 65 feet in length, while withstanding pressures up to 500 pounds per square inch (p.s.i.). The raft to be cured is placed in the autoclave and steam is introduced until the desired temperature and pressure are attained. These conditions are usually maintained from one to four hours until the rubber and adhesive are vulcanized. The pressure is then released and the raft removed. After cooling and cleaning, the vulcanized raft is ready.

In the case of thermal plastic coatings such as polyvinyl chloride or polyurethane, vulcanization is unnecessary. These polymers retain their characteristics through the normal air temperature range but become pliable at extremely high temperatures. Pieces are joined together by heat-sealing, which applies heat and pressure to the seam area, thus melting the plastic and bonding it together. Another method utilizes a solvent that chemically softens the coating and allows the two pieces to be joined together in the conventional manner.

TESTING

In either case the raft is visually inspected and over-pressured for burst strength (usually 5 to 8 p.s.i.) to test the integrity of the seams. The raft is subjected to a more lengthy test, usually twenty-four hours at normal operating pressures, in order to determine leakage.

A common standard of many inflatables purchased by the military requires that when the raft is inflated to 2 p.s.i., the air lost will be no greater than 0.5 p.s.i. in a twenty-four hour period. This simply means that during a day's run down the river, you do not have to worry about adding air.

Buying A River Raft

The number of raft models on the market has increased greatly in the last several years, and as a result, the decision of which raft to purchase can be complicated. This guide is designed to help simplify that decision. Factors to consider in purchasing a river raft are classified according to the following categories: dimensions, design, materials, and manufacturing techniques.

DIMENSIONS

The size of the raft needed presents the initial determination in purchasing a particular model. The length and width of the raft chosen will depend upon several factors—capacity for persons and gear, maneuverability, stability desired, and the type of river. For the private rafter, the typical length ranges from 12 to 16 feet, which is a good compromise for capacity, maneuverability, stability, and cost. Deciding upon the size of raft needed is complicated by the fact that the rafter may plan trips with different numbers of passengers, for various lengths of time, and on several rivers. It would be convenient to own several different sizes of rafts in order to fit the individual trip, but that option would prove costly, to say the least. A compromise must be made, then, and one must consider what size of raft will be required for the majority of trips, with alterations made for each trip.

Capacity for persons and gear is the first consideration affecting the size of raft chosen. A few generalizations may be made concerning capacities of river rafts used for whitewater runs. If gear is carried and a rowing frame used, a 6-man raft (12 ft. x 6 ft.) will accommodate two persons; a 7-man raft (13 ft. x 6½ ft.), three persons; a 10-man raft (15 ft. x 7½ ft.), four persons; and a 14-man raft (17 ft. x 8 ft.), five or six persons. If the raft is paddled instead of rowed, the capacity increases by two persons in the 10- and 14-man rafts and by one person in the 6- and 7-man rafts.

The amount of gear taken may depend both upon the personal preferences of the passengers and the length or type of trip. Longer trips, of course, will necessitate greater amounts of food, while cold weather trips will require more gear as a result of the additional clothing. Merely guessing how much gear a certain raft model will accommodate is imprecise at best; to determine the raft's capacity more accurately, it is preferable to inflate the raft under consideration and actually place gear into it. Usually there will be less room than you anticipate, due to the space taken up by the large buoyancy tubes of the raft. Overloading a raft can also present serious safety problems, for an overloaded raft is difficult to control and the possibility of losing gear is increased. The solution, obviously, is to choose either a larger model or reduce the amount of gear.

Despite the greater capacities of the larger rafts, maneuverability of these models requires more effort. For the most part, the larger and heavier the raft, the more difficult it is to maneuver. While the difference in maneuverability between a 12- and 13-foot raft is minimal, control becomes relatively more difficult in the 16- and 17-foot models. More physical strength is needed to row or paddle a larger raft and it requires greater anticipation and forethought to maneuver the raft through the rapids. A larger raft simply requires more time to move once a stroke is made.

Stability of the raft is yet another factor to be considered before purchasing a particular model, for a raft's size generally determines its stability. Large rapids may necessitate a larger and more stable raft, while those desiring a more adventurous ride should choose a shorter model. Although a longer boat is more stable than a shorter one, it is also more difficult to maneuver and requires more advance planning while running rapids. While it may require more skill to negotiate a smaller raft through large rapids without overturning, a smaller raft is also easier to maneuver if an obstacle is suddenly encountered.

The type of river floated may also dictate, to some extent, the size of the raft. Big volume rivers, or those with larger rapids, may require a longer boat that is more stable and not as prone prone to overturn. If the river is small and rocky, a small raft may become a necessity, since smaller rafts draw less water and are easier to maneuver between rocky stretches of the river.

DESIGN

Raft design involves more than mere appearance, for the size and shape of the buoyancy tubes, the number of air chambers, and the presence of cross tubes not only affect the handling characteristics of a raft, but contribute to its safety as well.

Size of buoyancy tubes. The buoyancy tube size of a raft is important for two reasons—the handling of the raft and the amount of water taken in during the rapids. Most rafts in the 12- to 14-foot range have tube sizes between 16 and 19 inches in diameter, while rafts of the 15- to 17-foot range have tubes between 18 and 21 inches. The 7-man surplus boats, as well as the newer paddle rafts patterned after them, employ smaller tubes, usually about 16 inches in diameter.

Buoyancy tube size may greatly affect handling characteristics of the raft because a larger tube, with its increased surface area, requires more effort to move and is therefore less responsive to an oar or paddle stroke than a smaller tube. A smaller tube is especially advantageous in a paddle raft, which is more difficult to maneuver than a raft steered by oars. The paddlers, too, are closer to the water and do not have to reach as far out of the raft to make a stroke.

The main advantage of a larger tube is its ability to prevent excessive amounts of water from coming into the raft, rendering it sluggish and almost impossible to control. A larger tube actually becomes a safety feature (with 16 inches as the minimum for safety). Paddle rafts with smaller tubes largely eliminate this problem by the use of an inflatable spray shield which surrounds the perimeter of the raft and blocks oncoming spray.

Bow and stern lift. The raised bow and stern feature has recently become popular. This uplift may be very pronounced (11 or 12 inches) in some models, but most are raised about 8 or 9 inches. This feature allows the raft to glide easier across the water once a stroke is made. It also aids in deflecting water from the raft.

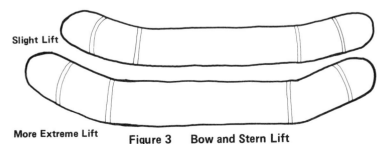

Slight Lift

More Extreme Lift   Figure 3   Bow and Stern Lift

Number of chambers. Multiple air chambers have become standard on most rafts. While some rafts contain two main chambers, most rafts in the 12- to 16-foot range incorporate four primary chambers, with supplemental chambers in the cross tubes. These multiple air chambers are an important safety feature: in case one chamber is torn and deflated, the other chambers will keep the raft afloat until the tear can be repaired.

Multiple air chambers also aid in the stability of a raft because the chambers reduce the shifting of air in the raft which occurs as it flexes through the waves of the rapids.

Cross tubes. Cross tubes, or thwarts, are also an important feature. They aid flotation and provide lateral stability to the raft. These tubes also provide places for passengers to sit, especially in vigorous rapids where the passengers need to move closer into the center of the raft to avoid falling out.

The primary disadvantage of cross tubes is the amount of space which they occupy, thus reducing gear capacity. To provide additional space for gear, some rafters inflate only the front cross tube and leave the rear cross tube uninflated.

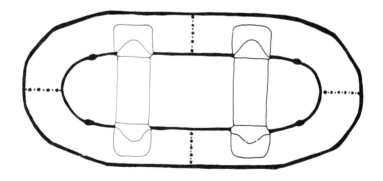

Figure 4   Air Chambers

Perforated lines indicate position of baffles (bulkheads).

MATERIALS

The type of material used in a raft has a definite relationship to the raft's retail price because as much as two-thirds of the manufacturing cost can be attributed to the material. The fabrics used in the manufacture of rafts offer several advantages and disadvantages which are listed in table 1.

The coatings bonded to the fabric are usually labeled with the terms "neoprene," "Hypalon," "polyvinyl chloride," or "polyurethane." These are simply generic names which encompass a wide variety of polymers within each group. For instance, there are more than twenty neoprene polymers, four Hypalons, and many polyurethanes available. Each of the basic polymers is compounded by adding different ingredients in varying amounts to achieve certain characteristics. Thus there are literally thousands of different compounds with different purposes.

All compounds, therefore, are a compromise. For example, in order to achieve hardness, or wear resistance, there is generally a resulting reduction in adhesion. It is impossible, then, to generalize concerning the desirability of a neoprene, Hypalon or polyurethane coating without knowing the characteristics of the particular compound used. Many of the so-called "Hypalons" contain a large percentage of neoprene or natural rubber, despite the indefinite label of "Hypalon."

Raft manufacturers will provide further specifications regarding the physical characteristics of their coated fabrics, such as fabric weights, thread denier, tensile and tear strength, and puncture resistance. References to these specifications, however, can be misleading, because they are basically relative. It is impossible to compare materials unless certain parameters of physical characteristics (such as minimum tensile and tear strength or puncture resistance) are established. As a result, only the actual physical characteristics of the finished fabric have any bearing on its ability to withstand the punishment of whitewater use. Do not be misled by labels: buy from a reliable manufacturer.

Valves. Large valves, such as the military high volume valves, are preferable, because they allow more air to be pumped into the raft in a shorter period of time. They also permit easier and quicker deflation. The Peters and Russel one-piece valve, as well as the I.T.T. and Campways valves, employ an integral design in which the valve does not separate from the valve core. Another excellent valve is the Bridgeport-Schraeder valve, which is a two-piece valve.

The valve core, of course, should be well attached to the raft, and neither it nor the valve should leak. Air leaks can be checked by wiping the valve and surrounding area with soapy water; any bubbles that appear indicate a leak.

Recessing of valves also is a desirable option, as it prevents gear from pushing against the valve and possibly causing a leak.

TABLE 1
Advantages and Disadvantages of Base Fabrics

Fabric	Advantages	Disadvantages
Cotton	Inexpensive	Subject to deterioration
	Easy to cut and assemble	Low tensile and tear strength
Nylon	Readily available	Heavier than Dacron polyester or DuPont Kevlar
	Will not deteriorate	Lower tensile and tear strength than Dacron polyester or DuPont Kevlar
	Relatively easy to cut and assemble	
	Less expensive than Dacron polyester or DuPont Kevlar	
Dacron Polyester	Approximately twice as strong as nylon for given fabric weight	Approximately twice the cost of nylon
	Can be cut and assembled easier than DuPont Kevlar	
DuPont Kevlar	Stronger than steel by weight	Approximately eight times the cost of nylon
	Extremely light weight	Difficult to cut
	Results in a raft that that is extremely rigid *	No stretch, making it difficult to assemble

*This rigidity is a debatable advantage. The question is whether the raft should remain extremely rigid or whether it should flex slightly to conform to the surface of the water.

Other Material. Other materials of the raft, such as its "D" rings, should be also noted. The best "D" rings are those made of welded stainless steel, while less expensive rings are cadmium-plated or galvanized. Accessories, such as a repair kit, spare valves, grab lines, and so forth, should also be checked.

MANUFACTURING PROCEDURES

The vast majority of inflatable boats are made by cutting panels from a coated fabric and then gluing them together. The seams of the boat become especially important because of the pressure exerted at this point, caused by the shifting of air inside the buoyancy tubes as the raft is compressed and extended through the rapids.

Seams used in the construction of rafts may be of several types. The principal methods include the lap seam and the butt seam. The lap seam is one in which one part of the material is laid over the top of the other approximately ¾ inch. The butt seam is where the two cut edges are brought together and taped inside and out to ensure air tightness.

The lap seam method provides greater strength and boat rigidity, but butt seams are fine if a wide seam tape is used. Three inch tape provides a good bond, as long as the correct vulcanizing or gluing procedures are followed. One should check the edges of the seam tape, making sure the seam tape has adhered to the raft without any gaps. Air bubbles in the seam tape also indicate areas where the adhesion is poor.

Since the selling price of a raft is only a rough indicator of the workmanship employed in its manufacture, ask other rafters and commercial outfitters about their experience with particular models. This way, you can determine the reputable and well-established manufacturers who will stand behind their warranties.

2

Rafting Equipment

Rafting equipment complements the function of the raft in river running. It renders the raft more riverworthy and its crew better prepared to meet the challenge of whitewater. Good quality equipment thus becomes a necessity. Fortunately, developments in the construction of rafts and the increased popularity of river running have brought about improvements in the designs and materials of rafting equipment.

Frames

A raft frame's primary function is to enable gear to be secured above the floor of the raft. If gear is left on the floor, a rock passing underneath the raft might possibly tear the floor, if it could not flex under stress. A frame is also a necessity when oars are used to row the raft, for the means of power and control require a rigid structure.

Light, simple frames are generally the best. They do the job well, are inexpensive, and easy to transport and store. Moreover, if wooden frames are assembled with carriage bolts, or if metal frames slip together, these frames may be broken down for easy transportation to the river.

A floorboard is often suspended from the frame by means of chains encased in a plastic hose. This floorboard provides additional space for gear to be lifted off of the raft's floor. To avoid the chance of a rock ripping the raft floor when jammed against the floorboard, this floorboard deck should never extend more than halfway down from the top of the buoyancy tubes.

For additional space a net may be strung across the stern and secured by "D" rings to form a poop deck. This poop deck also may consist of a rectangular or square frame with a suspended floorboard. Baggage is placed on the net or floorboard, a tarp laid over it, and then the bundle is securely lashed down with a line.

No set rules exist for constructing a frame: different frames are needed for different purposes. The frame chosen will depend upon such factors as the amount of gear, the use of oars or paddles, the wear of the frame on the raft, the position of the passengers, bailing methods, and the type of river. Personal preference also plays a subtle, but important, part in the decision.

The frame, in any event, should not hamper access to the valves of the raft, and easy bailing should be possible. Most importantly, the frame should be sufficiently sturdy to withstand the severe punishment of heavy rapids.

WOODEN FRAMES

Wooden frames offer several advantages. They are cheaper than metal frames and relatively easy to construct. The wooden frame may consist simply of a square or rectangle of 2 x 6s or 2 x 8s of pine or fir, with oar mounts of oak or metal. Carriage bolts can be used to bolt the frame together, allowing the frame to be easily dismantled. Nails should never be used in the frame, as they may puncture the raft if the frame is torn apart under impact. Wood is easy to work with and it is easier to replace from natural sources.

Several points should be noted in the construction of wooden frames:

- Span the frame from the top center of one side of the buoyancy tube to the top center of the other tube.
- Round the edges of the side rails of the frame to reduce abrasion of the frame against the raft.
- Sand the bottom of the frame smooth and pad areas of wear.
- Apply several coats of marine spar varnish or marine paint to the frame.
- Stagger bolts to prevent weakening of the boards.
- Recess all bolt nuts and heads.

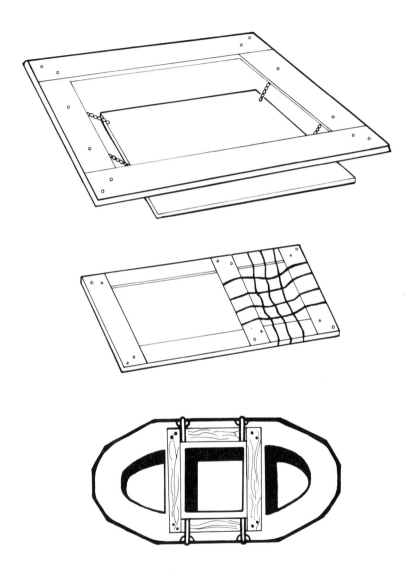

Figure 5   Wooden Frames

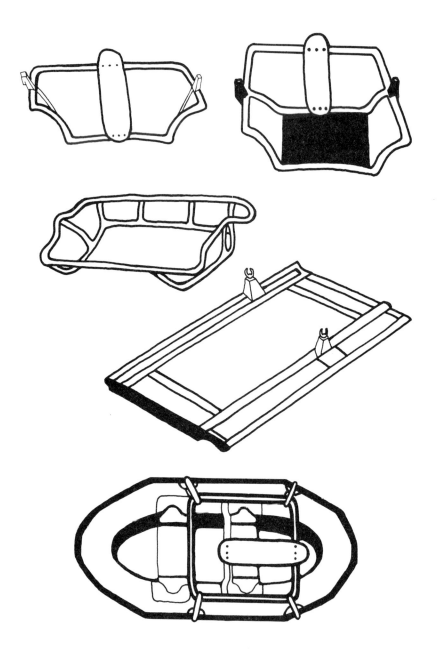

Figure 6   Metal Frames

METAL FRAMES

Rowing frames also may be made of metal, either small-diameter steel tubing or larger-diameter aluminum tubing. Aluminum's lightness and non-corrosive qualities make it an excellent frame material. The major disadvantage of aluminum is the difficulty and expense of heliarc welding (and its softness also limits its use somewhat). Steel, on the other hand, is less expensive, but is also heavier than aluminum. Steel will also rust unless painted with a suitable epoxy coating.

Metal frames are usually sturdier than wood frames although they are more expensive. The designs in ready-made metal frames have progressed a great deal in recent years, and breakdown frames are now available. Many of these models also incorporate ice chests into their design to be used as a rower's seat.

Pad as much of the frame's hard surface as possible with foam rubber to prevent possible injury if someone falls against the frame during an upset of the raft. Tiny bits of metal may result from the welding of a metal frame, so be sure to bevel off all corners of the frame to reduce unnecessary wear on the raft. Because a metal frame is more difficult to repair if the welding breaks, soft metal baling wire should be included in the repair kit for this possibility.

"D" RINGS

After the type of frame to be used is determined, the frame must be attached to the raft in some manner. The best method employs "D" rings which are mounted on the raft, with nylon webbing straps used to fasten the frame to the "D" rings. These "D" rings should be mounted mid-way down the outer side of the tube and not on top of the tube. This placement will allow the pull to remain at a right angle to the flat side of the "D" ring, thus preventing the "D" ring from tearing from the patch (by maximizing sheer tension and minimizing perpendicular tension).

Oars and Paddles

Oars and paddles are essential to propel the raft through calm water and control it in whitewater. After deciding whether to use oars or paddles, the rafter must choose among the different materials and various lengths currently available.

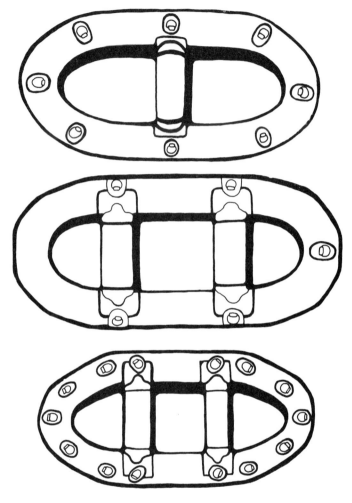

Figure 7   "D" Ring Placement

Placement varies according to type of frame and safety lines used.

OARS

River oars must be sturdy and long enough to withstand the rigors of whitewater rafting. Oars designed for river work feature long blades, normally spanning one-third the length of the entire oar. Wooden oars are the most commonly used. Spruce, though light and fairly strong, has a tendency to break. Painted oars, too, are usually of poor quality, as the paint is used to conceal structural defects. Cottonwood and basswood oars are adequate for light and medium duty use. They are less expensive than ash or oak oars and are fairly strong, especially when laminated.

Ash oars and those made of oak are generally considered the most durable. Although the shafts are very difficult to break, the blades of the oar may crack. To prevent this possibility, many boaters wrap the blades with fiberglass tape. For this reason, too, oars with ash shafts and plastic blades are now commercially available.

Despite their durability, ash oars are extremely heavy, as well as expensive. An ash oar is a solid oar so the woodworker must start with a full stud of high quality lumber. When producing a solid oar, the manufacturer cannot work around knots, as possible with a laminated oar. The solid oar also creates significant waste in certain areas of the oar, such as around the handles.

The best ash for the manufacture of oars is mountain grown, especially that of the Appalachian mountains, because ash grown at lower altitudes tends to be very limber. In fact, many laminated cottonwood oars are stiffer than bottom grown ash oars.

When selecting oars it is necessary to note whether the grain runs parallel to the shaft. Any grain running even slightly crossways to the shaft indicates a potentially weak area. The shaft should be thick and strong at the throat, the point where the blade meets the shaft. To test an oar, hold it at about a forty-five degree angle with one hand and apply pressure with the foot about halfway up the oar. Some flexibility is fine, but too much indicates a poor quality oar.

Several recent developments have occurred in the manufacture of oars with aluminum shafts and plastic blades. These developments have been made with good reason, for aluminum oars are extremely durable and lightweight as compared with good quality ash oars. Wooden oars have a tendency to warp in storage, a problem not present with aluminum oars. The cost of good ash oars has also increased so rapidly in recent years that aluminum oar prices are competitive, or in some instances less, with ash oars.

The length of oars used for rafting will vary according to the length of the raft: generally, oar length is approximately two-thirds of the length of the raft. Therefore, most 12-foot rafts will use 8- or 9-foot oars; 14-foot rafts, 9- or 10-foot oars; and 16-foot rafts, 10- or 11-foot oars. Heavier loads and larger rapids will necessitate longer oars, and low volume and rocky rivers will require slightly shorter oars to aid maneuverability in tight stretches of the river.

The distance between the oarlocks will also affect the length of oar chosen, for the oarlocks should be correctly positioned on the oar shaft in order to obtain the most effective fulcrum point for easy rowing. Oarlocks will be mounted on the middle of the buoyancy tubes so they should be placed about a third down the length of the oar measuring from the handles. When the oars, equipped with oarlocks, are lifted out of the water, the handles of the oars should remain several inches apart to avoid pinching the hands while rowing.

The handles of oars may present possibilities for developing blisters. These blisters can be prevented by sanding the handles of wooden oars to ensure perfect smoothness. Adhesive tape may be wound around the handles to reduce chafing. Plastic sleeves that slip over the handles of the oars to provide a more comfortable grip are also available.

Even good quality oars are easily broken, so it is necessary to exercise a few precautions to prevent possible damage to the oars. Never use oars to fend off rocks, even to avert a collision, and be especially careful to avoid jamming the downstream oar against a rock. In rocky streams it is best to take quick, shallow strokes. Use smooth, steady strokes to prevent breaking an oar while rowing.

Oars may also fall into the river if separated from the thole pin or oarlock. This can occur when the oar hits an obstacle and the clip is forced off of the thole pin, or it can simply slip through the round oarlock or oarhorn. To avoid losing oars, secure each oar with a strong, light nylon line, and tie one end of the line to the oar shaft slightly below the clip or oarlock and the other end of the line to the rowing frame.

It is advisable to carry two spare oars due to the possibility of breakage or loss. These spare oars are usually suspended horizontally on the side of the raft, tied closely to the frame with nylon line.

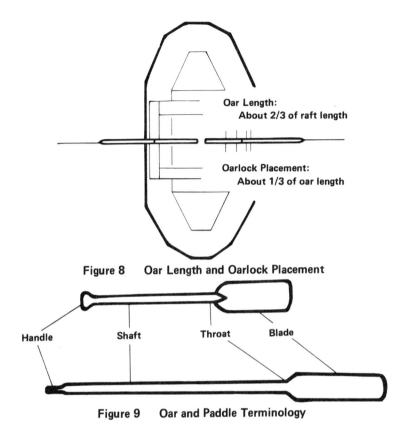

Figure 8   Oar Length and Oarlock Placement

Oar Length:
About 2/3 of raft length

Oarlock Placement:
About 1/3 of oar length

Handle   Shaft   Throat   Blade

Figure 9   Oar and Paddle Terminology

PADDLES

Many different types and brands of paddles have recently become available. These paddles, manufactured with different combinations of materials, differ according to such factors as flexibility, weight, and cost. As a result, paddles have become a complicated subject for the racing canoeist or kayaker. The needs of rafters, however, are less exacting.

The materials from which a paddle is made determine how that particular paddle will handle. Wood, of course, is the oldest, time-proven material. Wood has good compression and tensile strength, and a good feel that "gives" with the stroke. Lamination also provides an excellent strength-to-weight ratio and is resistant to minor nicks and dents. Wood does not assume extremes of temperature, thus providing a more comfortable paddle to hold, especially in cold weather.

Wood does have its disadvantages. Hardwood paddles, although tough, are heavy and tiring to use, while softwood paddles, lighter in weight, are not as durable. Wood absorbs small amounts of water that render the paddle heavier and weaker, so a good finish must be maintained to prevent rot and delamination. Also check to make sure the grain runs straight and the shaft and throat are thick and strong. Wrapping the tip of the paddle with fiberglass tape will prevent further splintering and greatly prolong the life of the paddle.

Several newer models of paddles feature blades manufactured with fiber-reinforced plastic. The fibers may be fiberglass or DuPont Kevlar, or a combination of the two, while the plastics are commonly polyester or epoxy. Other paddles have blades of the thermoplastics, such as ABS plastic or polypropylene. All of these blades are extremely durable, lightweight, and consistent in quality.

Shafts for these paddle blades are ordinarily aluminum or epoxy-fiberglass. Aluminum is strong, lightweight, inexpensive, and easy to form into an oval shape for more comfortable hand grips. The best aluminum shafts are made of a seamless alloy, while less expensive shafts with welded seams are usually thicker and heavier. Aluminum, however, is very cold to the touch, but a plastic, neoprene, or fiberglass wrap will protect the shaft and provide insulation for the paddler's hands.

An increasing number of paddle shafts are manufactured with fiberglass-epoxy materials, such as those used in fiberglass pole vaults. These shafts are very strong and lightweight with a flexibility similar to wood. The hand grips, however, cannot be easily molded into a comfortable oval shape, and attachment of the blade to the shaft often creates manufacturing problems.

For rafting, durability and cost are prime factors in selecting paddles. The newer paddles with thermoplastic blades and aluminum shafts seem ideal, because they are very inexpensive and almost unbreakable.

Paddle length depends on several factors. In addition to personal preference, these factors include the size of the raft's tubes, height of the paddler, and position of the paddler in the raft. The normal range includes lengths from 4½ to 6 feet, with 5 and 5½ feet as the most common. Rafts with smaller tubes (16 to 18 inches) will necessitate shorter lengths, while the 20 inch and larger tubes will probably require at least 5 foot paddles.

The height of the paddler may *help* determine the size that is most comfortable to use. The paddle should not be so short that the paddler must lean out of the raft to make a stroke, nor should the paddle be so long that the stroke is executed with the arms above the head.

The position of the paddler is also important in the determination of paddle length. A paddler in the bow straddling the tubes has only a short distance to reach and thus may use a shorter paddle. The boater in the middle of the stern, however, needs a longer paddle to steer and make draw strokes to turn the raft.

Oarlocks

An important decision for the rowing rafter involves the type of oarlocks used. Generally, oarlocks can be classified into four categories: oarhorns, round oarlocks, thole pins and clips, and clamp-on models.

OARHORNS

The oarhorn is the most basic oarlock, and it can be used with or without a pin or carriage bolt that passes through the oar and fastens to the oarlock.

With pins. When used with a pin, the oarhorn enables the oar to move up and down by rotating on the pin, but the blade of the oar remains fixed at a perpendicular angle. This type of oarhorn is easy to row because there is no concern with the movement of the blade angle.

The primary disadvantage of this oarhorn is the weakening of the oar shaft that occurs when a hole is drilled to accommodate the oarlock pin. While this drilling may cause only a minimal effect on the strength of the oar, it is possible that the oar will be seriously weakened by the drilling. Any weakening which may occur as a result of this drilling can be minimized by wrapping fiberglass tape around the oar where the pin is to be placed.

This oarhorn does not allow the oars to be pulled into the raft, so if the oar hits a rock, the oar may break at the throat where it is attached to the oarlock.

Without pins. When the oarhorn is used without pins, the oar is usually wrapped with neoprene, fiberglass, or nylon cord in order to protect the oar from chafing against the oarlock. An oar stopper may be used to prevent the oar from slipping through the oarlock and into the river if the rower loses grip of the oar. The oar stopper is usually a circular fastener made of rubber or plastic and secured by radiator hose clips or carriage bolts.

The advantage of using an oarhorn without a pin is the ability to pull the oars out of the water and into the raft, especially when floating through narrow or rocky stretches of the river. This oarlock also allows the oars to be feathered by adjusting the angle of the blade in the water. The need to drill holes in the oar to retain a pin, as well as its potential weakening of the oar shaft, is also eliminated.

The main disadvantage of the oarhorn without pins is the conscious effort required to insure that the blade remains at the correct angle in the water because difficult rapids make it impossible to concentrate on adjusting the blade angle. Although this changing movement of the blade is annoying to many rowers, the protective sleeve that covers the oar at the oarlock reduces much of this free movement.

ROUND OARLOCKS

Round oarlocks are almost identical to the oarhorn without pins, but instead they completely encircle the oar. As with the oarhorn, the oar is wrapped with neoprene, fiberglass, or nylon cord in order to prevent chafing of the oar, and the oar cannot slide out of the oarlock if an oar stopper is used.

The advantages of the round oarlock include the ability to feather the oar blades and to ship the oars into the raft if necessary. Pins are not used so there is no need to drill holes in the oar.

THOLE PINS AND CLIPS

Thole pins and clips, although the most expensive oarlock, are very popular among rafters in the West. Attached perpendicularly to the raft frame, the thole pin is a metal rod containing a nylon bushing. A clip fits snugly around this bushing so the clip can move with the bushing around the pin. The oar is attached to the clip by means of radiator hose clips.

The blade of the oar is held in a fixed position by the clip, and drilling holes in the oar is unnecessary. If the oar hits a rock in the river, the clip will pop off the bushing without breaking the oar at the oarlock. The oar should always be positioned in front of the thole pin in order to reduce unnecessary stress on the clip.

The thole pin may present some safety problems, however, if a passenger falls on top of the pin, or if the raft overturns with the pin protruding. This hazard may be reduced somewhat by attaching foam rubber balls on top of the pins.

CLAMP-ON MODEL

Although its use is not yet widespread, the clamp-on model is probably the most recent development in oarlocks. Simple in design, this oarlock fits closely around the oar and is tightened by bolts, eliminating the need for drilling holes in the oar.

Many reports regarding this type of oarlock recommend it only for light or medium duty use. This limited use is probably due to the type of materials employed in its manufacture and not its design. If a stronger alloy metal were used, this would appear to be an excellent oarlock, for it eliminates the weakening of the oar caused by drilling and at the same time provides a fixed oar blade position.

OTHER CONSIDERATIONS FOR OARLOCKS

Oarlocks should be manufactured from high quality metals, since there is a great deal of stress exerted at this point. Manganese bronze and silicone bronze oarlocks are very sturdy, as well as others made of strong alloy metals. These oarlocks can even be pounded back into shape if they are forced open by pressure of the oar. Pot metal oarlocks are usually not satisfactory for heavy whitewater, as they crack easily under force.

Spare oars should be equipped with oarlocks. If an oar is lost or broken, the spare oar can be placed immediately into the oarlock socket or on the thole pin and control is quickly regained. It is also advisable to keep a spare oarlock in the repair kit in the event that an oarlock is lost or damaged beyond repair.

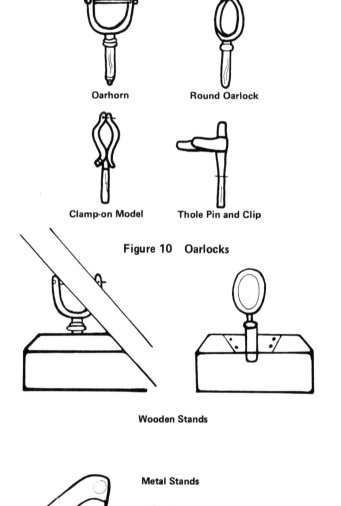

Oarhorn   Round Oarlock

Clamp-on Model   Thole Pin and Clip

Figure 10   Oarlocks

Wooden Stands

Metal Stands

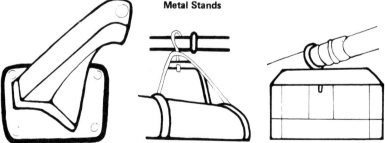

Figure 11   Oarlock Stands

OARLOCK STANDS

Several types of oarlock stands are available. The simplest arrangement is a hole drilled in a 4 or 6 inch square hardwood post which is mounted on the siderails of a wooden frame. If desired, metal sockets may be placed in these holes. Another socket design attaches to the outside of this block of wood, and these are satisfactory if securely bolted (not screwed or nailed) to the block.

A more recent oarlock stand model, made of metal and bolted to a wooden frame, is extremely durable. Many aluminum and steel frames contain a similar type of oarlock stand.

To ensure proper oar leverage and control, oarlock stands should be positioned slightly closer to the rear of the raft. Although many stands support the oarlocks in a vertical position, it is preferable if the oarlocks are offset with a ten to fifteen degree outward tilt for correct oar alignment.

Air Pumps

Air pumps used to inflate rafts, and sometimes deflate them, vary according to their method of inflation and amount of volume. To inflate a raft at the beginning of a trip, either a large volume barrel-style pump or electric model will provide quick inflation. Inflating an entire raft with a small hand pump is pure agony, to say the least. A foot pump that is operated by stepping on an accordion-like pump and releasing it in successive turns is somewhat better than a hand pump for initial inflation.

If a power source is available, electric pumps provide the easiest method of inflation. Some operate on electric current, while others can be plugged into a cigarette lighter or clipped to a car battery. One of these electric models contains a motor with one full horsepower capable of producing 60 cubic feet of air per minute. This model, amazingly, can inflate a 17-foot raft to a pressure of 3 pounds per square inch in less than five minutes. Other less expensive models are also available but are not as fast nor as high pressure.

Another method of inflation is a large barrel pump of the military style, normally 18 to 20 inches high and 6 inches in diameter. These pumps usually have two foot pedals for stability while pumping, and many models have two hoses, thus allowing the inflation of two raft chambers at the same time.

These large cylinder pumps are fairly expensive so it pays to check out the features of the individual model carefully. The number of parts in the pump is a crucial factor. The number varies widely from 25 in one model to more than 100 in others. Generally, the fewer parts, the better. There are two reasons for this: there is less of a possibility of malfunction, and assembly and disassembly time are reduced. With fewer parts, the pump can be completely disassembled in two or three minutes. The simplicity of some models also requires nothing more than a screwdriver to take the pump apart.

Note the number of metal and die cast parts. Only a minimum number of metal parts should be used, for they will corrode if wet. A good cylinder pump contains components which, for the most part, can be easily obtained at a local hardware store (in addition to their availability from the pump factory).

Check the total volume, measured in cubic inches, of the various models. The volume will normally vary between 300 and 400 cubic inches, and the larger the volume, the quicker the inflation of the raft.

Find out if the pump is immersible, which will prevent water from damaging the internal workings of the pump. Most pumps with metal fittings within the pump will corrode and rust if wet and therefore are not immersible. An immersible pump may even serve as an efficient bilge pump in a pinch.

Also check to see if the pump is reversible, allowing deflation as well as inflation. This reversibility is a desirable feature because it relieves the frustration of removing the air from a raft before storage.

Lastly, but most importantly, select a model that pumps easily. Foot pumps, which vary in quality and volume, are much easier to operate for a long period of time than a hand pump. The better makes contain strong springs, durable hinges, and steel-reinforced sides.

A small volume hand pump is necessary for topping off the raft because most rafts will lose some air during the day and require inflation each morning before another day's run. These hand pumps, twelve inches long and three inches in diameter, are compact and easily carried. The pumps usually contain fittings that either screw or fit closely into the valve of the raft, thus allowing a high pressure to be attained.

Waterproof Containers

To protect clothes, food, first aid kits, and other rafting and camping equipment from spray that enters the raft, waterproof containers—in the form of bags and boxes—become a necessity.

WATERPROOF BAGS

Military surplus rubber bags, once used to protect photographic, communications, and medical supplies, are used by rafters as waterproof containers. These black bags vary in size, but all are extremely durable. Most of these surplus bags require closing the lips of the bag together to form a seal, which is then folded over several times and fastened down by straps to prevent the entry of water.

These surplus bags are excellent for storage of clothes, food, and kitchen utensils. When used for kitchen utensils, a cardboard box may be slipped inside to provide organization and easier access to the contents.

Unfortunately, surplus bags have become scarce and are now difficult to obtain. Most rafting supply stores and catalogs, however, now offer a complete line of waterproof bags. Several of these new models are patterned after the military surplus bags, but other new designs are available. Waterproof duffle bags, made of neoprene- or Hypalon-reinforced nylon, are especially suited for the protection of clothes. These bags usually contain a flap extending about ten inches from the top of the bag. This flap is bunched together and tied before it is stuffed inside the bag; then the drawstring is tightened to close the seal.

Rectangular bags, made of polyethylene or polypropylene, are less expensive than rubber bags and yet remain fairly durable. These bags are usually sealed by means of a tubular clamp that slides across the edges of the bag opening.

The least expensive arrangement incorporates a plastic bag (such as a heavy-duty garbage bag or trash compactor bag) that is placed inside a nylon duffle bag. The top of the plastic bag should be bunched together and folded over several times before it is tied. This system allows the inner plastic bag to repel water while the outer nylon bag protects against abrasion.

Smaller bags, ordinarily about 18 by 12 inches in dimension and constructed of rubber or heavy vinyl material, are excellent as ditty bags to store items needed occasionally during the day. These bags often seal by folding the flap over several times and then snapping several fasteners.

These small bags may also be used as camera containers if lined with a layer of foam rubber or Ensolite for added protection. Newer models of these vinyl bags contain inflatable chambers on both sides of the bag. These chambers offer a protective cushioning for the camera and provide flotation, if the bag should be tossed overboard.

WATERPROOF BOXES

The most popular type of waterproof box for river use is the military surplus ammunition container. These ammo boxes are available in various sizes at most surplus stores. The rubber sealing gasket in the lid, however, should be checked carefully for defects and water tightness by immersing the closed box in water and vigorously flexing the sides several times. Any air bubbles rising from the box indicate leaks. After this test is completed, the box should only contain a few drops of water which have entered as the box is opened. If the box does leak, replacement of the entire box is preferable to changing the sealing gasket. These boxes may also be painted white or aluminum color to reduce heat buildup.

In addition to surplus boxes, several models of fiberglass and metal waterproof boxes are commercially available. Wooden boxes may also be made specifically for this purpose. To ensure water tightness, the edges should be fiberglassed or caulked and weatherstripping inserted around the lid of the box.

Plastic boxes with snap-on lids, similar to those commonly used by restaurants to store pickles, mustard, and mayonnaise, are also an inexpensive method of waterproofing gear. These are exceptionally lightweight, and the lid is pressed down around the entire rim of the container for a perfectly watertight seal.

Waterproof boxes can be used for waterproofing any piece of gear, but they are most commonly used for food, kitchen utensils and cookware, first aid supplies, and repair kits. These boxes are also fine for camera storage and protection. The surplus ammunition boxes are especially protective for camera equipment when lined with foam rubber or Ensolite. For some of the small pocket cameras, a widemouth plastic bottle will suffice, especially when equipped with a rubber gasket. Wrapping the camera in a wool sock absorbs any spurious water and reduces damage from scratches and shock.

RIGGING THE GEAR

Rigging and tying down the raft's gear is important from both a convenience and a safety standpoint. Personal items needed during the day, such as cameras, sunglasses, suntan oil, and perhaps a poncho, should be placed in small bags or boxes which are easily accessible. A first aid kit and air pump also should be handy. Lunch may be packed into a similar container for easy access. Once the empty raft has been placed in the river, the large boxes and bags containing food, clothing, and other gear can be loaded into the raft and lashed down securely.

Lashing the gear down firmly is especially important to personal safety, for loose gear in heavy rapids can hit and injure passengers. If correctly tied down, the gear should not be lost, even in a complete flip. A properly loaded raft also maneuvers more easily through the rapids.

Pack the gear so the load is as low as possible, utilizing the floorboard and poop deck. None of the gear should protrude from the sides of the raft, and the load should not interfere with rowing or paddling. The load should be balanced as evenly as possible on both sides of the raft.

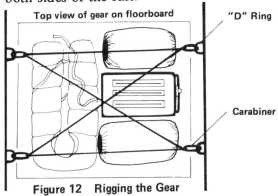

Top view of gear on floorboard   "D" Ring

Carabiner

Figure 12   Rigging the Gear

Soft items, such as waterproof bags, should be placed close together on the floorboard or poop deck, covered with a tarp and tied down securely. Ammo boxes and other hard box containers should be equipped with carabiners or nylon webbing straps with buckles. These carabiners and webbing can then be fastened to short lines on the frame or to "D" rings on the raft to prevent these containers from taking flight in rapids.

Life Jackets

A life jacket is an absolute necessity as a safeguard for the possibility of falling out of the raft and into the rapids. Most people do not maintain enough natural buoyancy to stay afloat, so a life jacket is needed to keep the head and chin above water.

The river runners of the 20s and 30s used life preservers made of cork, and later the inflatable "Mae West" jackets of World War II became popular. Today life jackets approved by the U.S. Coast Guard are categorized into four types, Type I, II, III, and V, classified according to how they move the wearer in the water.

The Type I Personal Flotation Device (PFD) has the greatest buoyancy requirements and is required for commercial vessels; the Type II Buoyant Vest is designed for recreational use. Both Type I and II provide a "positive righting movement," which has the effect of turning an unconscious wearer from a face-down position onto his back and then into a face-up position. This "righting" characteristic is especially beneficial to one who might be rendered unconscious when hitting a rock in the rapids.

Type III Buoyant Devices were designed to provide the greatest amount of comfort and mobility. They are described as providing a "stable, upright position" that maintains a person in an upright to slightly backward position, with no tendency to put him in a face-down position.

Type IV is a buoyant seat cushion—but this type is not recommended for river running.

Type V is an open category which is reserved by the Coast Guard for specific and restricted use. Several companies have begun manufacturing Type V jackets primarily for whitewater use.

Most life jackets are made of either kapok or closed-cell foam. Kapok, widely used in Type I and II jackets, is a vegetable fiber grown on trees in tropical countries. The kapok fiber has a wax-like coating that provides the buoyancy of the jacket, and it is enclosed in sealed vinyl packets to protect the coating. Once these packets are punctured or compressed, the kapok will deteriorate and mildew, with a resulting lack of buoyancy. Periodically check the air tightness of these packets by simply squeezing them to make sure the compartments are firm.

A closed cell foam, ordinarily either polyvinyl chloride (PVC) or polyethylene (such as Ensolite), is most commonly used in Type III and V jackets. This foam is relatively dense so it can be used in the construction of durable and comfortable life jackets.

Regardless of the type of life jacket used, it should be worn at all times. The buckles and clips should be securely fastened, not only to ensure that the jacket will stay on, but to avoid entangling the straps with the frame in an upset. A dangerous situation can occur if the wearer is entrapped by these straps under an overturned raft.

Other Equipment

Other rafting equipment is needed: rope, for raft lines, gear tie-downs, and rescue uses; bail buckets, to remove water from the raft; and channel-locks, a pump-type pliers whose uses are seemingly unlimited.

Rope. In addition to its use as a bow line, stern line, and gear lashings, rope is necessary for lining the raft around impassable rapids and for emergency rescues of rafts and persons. The length of the rope depends primarily upon the severity of the river—the more dangerous the river, the more rope necessary. For an average trip, carry a 50-foot and a 100-foot hank. Attach the 50-foot line to the bow of the raft. For quick tie-ups, the 50-foot length eliminates the trouble of handling excess rope. The 100-foot rope can be tied to the stern for more remote tie-ups and for a second tie-up at night. (It is also advisable to carry several large tent stakes in the event that good, secure lashing points are unavailable.) The longer length of the 100-foot rope is also necessary for lining and rescue work. On more dangerous rivers where lining and rescue are even remotely possible, a 200-foot rope should be included.

Ropes vary according to energy absorption, stretch, water absorption, resistance to deterioration, and resistance to abrasion. The rope chosen should be sufficiently strong in any case, but various materials are now available. In addition to the traditional manila, ropes are manufactured of polypropylene, nylon, polyester, or a combination of these materials. Manila is relatively cheap and strong, but it absorbs water easily, and its stiffness makes it somewhat difficult to handle.

Photo courtesy of Campways

Polypropylene is light and will not rot, and its ability to float renders it excellent as a rescue throw rope. Its main disadvantage is the tendency of knots to slip—the result of its slippery surface.

Nylon, with its flexibility, handles well and holds knots securely. Its disadvantage is the characteristic to stretch under stress and to whip dangerously if it breaks. A good quality nylon rope, however, will have a high tensile strength that will rarely break.

Polyester wears longer with good abrasion resistance, and it is less expensive than other materials. It is not as strong as polypropylene or nylon and should not be used with larger rafts or on violent rivers.

The best ropes incorporate the advantages of each material. For example, combining a polypropylene core with a nylon or polyester sheath produces a strong, easy-to-handle rope that also floats.

Bail Buckets. Great amounts of water may enter the raft and render it sluggish. A bail bucket is needed to remove that water. Bailers should be made of heavy plastic, and they can vary in capacity from one to three gallons. The three-gallon size is the best for rivers with large rapids that require bailing large quantities of water. Due to the weight, buckets larger than three gallons are difficult to handle (because water weighs about eight pounds per gallon). A one-gallon bucket can be used to reach small amounts of water that enter the raft.

Replace the metal handles of the bucket with more durable nylon cord. Clip the bucket to the frame or a "D" ring by means of a carabiner to prevent losing it. As a safety precaution, carry a spare bail bucket.

Channel Lock Pliers. Channel lock pliers are probably the most versatile tool available for river work, and they eventually become almost indispensable. Their uses include, but are not limited to:

• Assembling bolts on frames.
• Tightening and loosening sticky raft valves.
• Carrying hot cookware and lifting Dutch oven lids.
• Repairing the raft including rolling down patches, pulling off old patches.

3

Running Rapids

The key to running rapids successfully requires an understanding of the river itself—its currents, form, and flow. This knowledge of the river can then be applied to a knowledge of rowing or paddling techniques, allowing the rafter to negotiate the raft without mishap through a clear passage of the rapids.

Rapids

The river has many moods: the flatwater stretches provide stillness and serenity, while whitewater offers challenge and excitement. Although the quiet stretches of the river are as important to the rafter's experience as the rapids, the composition of rapids is more complicated, requiring a thorough understanding of their forces.

PHYSICAL CHARACTERISTICS

Rapids are actually caused by a number of factors, including the physical characteristics of the riverbed and the volume of the river. The most obvious physical characteristic contributing to the development of rapids is the roughness of the riverbed, formed by rocks and boulders that have fallen from surrounding mountains or canyons or that have been swept into the main current by the flow of adjoining sidestreams.

The gradient of the river, as it flows downstream, also causes the water to move faster, which renders the rapids more difficult to maneuver. This gradient is typically measured in terms of the average number of feet per mile the river drops. Generally, the greater the drop, the more dangerous the river.

As with any generalization, exceptions exist. Many rivers, most notably the Colorado River through the Grand Canyon, have mild gradients because of the long stretches of calm water which drop suddenly into tremendous rapids. Other rivers, however, feature high gradients, but the gradient is so uniform, or the riverbed is so smooth, that the river is easy to maneuver.

But roughness and gradient of the riverbed are not the only factors that contribute to the formation of the rapids. Constriction of the river current also plays an important part. This constriction can result either from the narrowing of the river banks or the presence of large boulders; both confine the river to a more restricted course. Constriction of the river, then, has the corresponding effect of increasing the velocity of the river flow.

RIVER VOLUME

The volume of the river has a definite effect on the structure of the rapids. A large volume of water increases the speed of the river and the force of the rapids, reducing maneuvering time, and magnifying the consequences of emergencies. Generally, the greater the volume, the more difficult the rapids become. This is not always the case. At low water a rock may be clearly seen and avoided. At slightly higher water it may be possible to float over the rock which has created only a small wave. At even higher water levels, the rock may create a reversal that must be avoided. At still higher water levels, the reversal created by the rock may be completely washed out.

River volume is usually measured in terms of cubic feet per second (c.f.s.), which is simply the amount of water passing a specified point every second. This measurement is relative of course: a smaller riverbed requires less volume to become satisfactory for rafting than a larger river.

The volume of a free-flowing river also fluctuates greatly in the course of a year. Peak flows of snow-fed rivers typically occur during spring run-off, gradually decreasing throughout the summer and early fall but increasing somewhat during rainfalls. When running unknown rivers, always consult the proper river authorities concerning river volume and the suitability for rafting.

RAPIDS RATINGS

To rate both the difficulty of rivers and individual rapids, two scales have been established (see table 2). The European scale (known as the International Scale of River Difficulty) is the most universal scale in existence. It contains ratings of I to VI, and is used to describe either specific rapids or the entire section of a river. The American scale, on the other hand, ranges from 1 to 10 and is used primarily on the large Western rivers for the rating of individual rapids.

These scales, however, should be regarded for what they are —general guidelines subject to change. A number of factors can alter these ratings. Changing river levels, for example, can greatly affect these ratings. Note the results of the changes in river level upon the rapids ratings in Hell's Canyon of the Snake River:

Rapids	Low Water Level	High Water Level
Wildsheep	7	9
Waterspout	8	6
Sluice Creek	6	7
Wild Goose	5	5

In some instances, the rising water level increases the rating. In other instances, the rapids become easier to run in high water, and in still other rapids, the level of difficulty remains the same. Most rapids, however, are more difficult in higher water, simply because the speed and force of the current are increased.

Cold water temperature (below 50 degrees Fahrenheit) or extended trips into the wilderness areas will cause these ratings to be understated. Beginners should note that these ratings are oriented toward boaters with previous river running experience.

Reading Whitewater

Not even the most powerful crew can overcome the river; safe passage is allowed only when the raft cooperates with the river's flow. Much of river running involves simply learning which portions of the river to avoid. The consequences of failing to avoid

TABLE 2
The Rapids Rating System

European	American	Description of Rapids	Experience Necessary
I	1,2	Moving water with a few riffles and small waves. Passages are clear with few or no obstructions. Very little maneuvering is required.	Easy: Practiced Beginner
II	3,4	Easy rapids with regular waves up to three feet. Wide, clear channels are obvious with scouting. Some maneuvering is required.	Requires Care: Intermediate Skill
III	5,6	Rapids with high, irregular waves. Passages are clear but narrow and may require scouting from the shore. Complex maneuvering may be required.	Difficult: Experienced
IV	7,8	Long rapids with powerful and irregular waves. Constricted passages usually require scouting from the shore. Precise maneuvering is required, and rescue is often difficult.	Very Difficult: Highly Skilled
V	9,10	Extremely large and violent rapids. Highly congested routes almost always require scouting from the shore. Critical and complex maneuvering is required. Rescue conditions are difficult and a significant hazard to life exists in the event of a mishap.	Exceedingly Difficult: Team of Experts
VI		Limits of navigation. Nearly impossible and very dangerous. Severe risk to life.	Utmost Difficulty: Team of Experts Taking Every Precaution

these obstacles vary. The raft may only be slightly jolted, or it may become filled with water. Large river hazards may hold the raft in place, preventing further movement downstream. More damaging, the raft may be torn or completely overturned.

TONGUE OF THE RAPIDS

When a river tilts downstream and still water turns white, the current is usually the fastest and deepest in the center. The friction between the water and the sides and bottom of the riverbed slows the current in the shallow sections, but in the deeper sections the current is swifter and more powerful. This power of the current clears rocks from the main channel and creates the characteristic "V" shaped lead-in at the head of the rapids. This "V" usually points to the deepest and least obstructed channel.

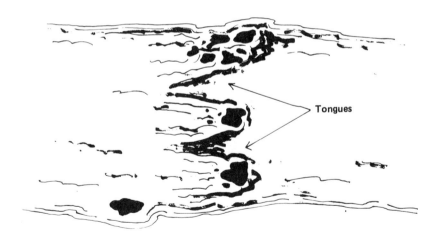

Figure 13   Tongue of the Rapids

REVERSALS

Rocks that protrude above the surface of the river are easy to spot. But when the water flows over the top of the rock and into the slack water behind it, the water creates a backflow as it moves upstream and back upon itself. This reversal of the river's current appearing downstream from a rock is generally known as a reversal.

When the rock is barely underwater, it is difficult to spot from upstream because there is little turbulence on the downstream side of the rock. Look for a calm spot in the midst of turbulence; the rock will partially deflect the current, and the water will remain level as it sweeps over the rock. If viewing the reversal from the shore, the downstream side of these rocks may be clearly visible. Other rocks, however, are concealed by spray and can be detected only by steady concentration.

If the rock is deeply submerged, a large reversal, commonly known as a hole (because of its appearance) may develop. The deeper the hole, the further upstream lies the rock. Large holes can easily flip a raft and should be avoided if possible. If the hole is unavoidable, approach it with the bow of the raft first, taking special care not to drift sideways into the hole.

Figure 14   Reversal

STANDING WAVES

Water moves swiftly over steep sections and slows down on more gradual inclines. When a fast section is followed by a slower one, the water piles up faster than it can be carried away. When the transition is gradual, this occurrence creates turbulence in the form of standing waves. The size of standing waves increases with the severity of the drop and the volume of water.

While standing waves are found, in some form, throughout most rapids, most are too small to cause concern. If the wave is high, but gradual, approach it bow first, allowing the raft to rise over the crest. If the waves are steep and angular, with either the chance of overturning the raft or filling it with great quantities of water, move to either side of the waves, which is usually more gradual than its center.

Make sure, however, that the waves are, in fact, standing waves. Rocks just below surface level can create mounds of water which first appear to be standing waves. Careful observation is required: standing waves are regular and patterned, while the waves concealing submerged rocks are usually jumbled.

BENDS

The study of the currents on a bend in the river is extremely important. Generally, the deepest and fastest current is along the outside of the bend. The flow of the water has a tendency to move the raft to the outside of the bend, which often contains large boulders and other hazards.

Considering the force of the currents, then, it is important to maintain the proper position and angle when entering a bend in the river. Approaching the rapids from the inside of the bend allows the option of moving easily to the outside of the bend and joining the main flow of the current. Approaching from the outside of the bend requires movement across the force of the current to the inside, if it is necessary to do so. The force of the current, however, can make this movement extremely difficult.

EDDIES

An eddy is a current that runs contrary to the direction of the river's main flow. Eddies generally move upstream behind rocks in the river or projections of the river's bank. The slack water on the inside of a bend in the river is also referred to as an eddy, even though this water does not flow upstream. The line between the main current and the eddy is known as the eddy fence (or eddy line). This eddy fence, in some cases, can be very powerful with the capability of moving the raft upstream.

Figure 15   Eddies

Eddies are useful currents when entering or leaving the shore, and they can be used to stop the raft while running rapids or establishing rescue stations. Some eddies, especially those of the swirling, whirlpool variety, are very powerful and should be avoided. Some eddies may even trap a raft and rotate it for hours.

Planning A Course

The obstacles and currents of many rapids can be seen clearly from upstream, but rapids that do not offer a complete view of their features should be scouted from the shore. Beach the raft well upstream and walk down to study the rapids ahead. As you walk down the side of the rapids, check carefully for rocks hidden from the view upstream, and rocks that are just below the surface of the water. These rocks are the most difficult to spot without steady concentration.

In viewing the rapids from either the river or shore, note the tongue of the rapids and the best point of entry. If entered correctly, many rapids require little or no maneuvering. Determine the direction of the main current in each section of the rapids, and note the river hazards along the route. Select the simplest and most direct route that follows the current and avoids obstacles. In deciding upon a particular course, consider the consequences of making a mistake and choose the route offering the least possibility of serious mishap.

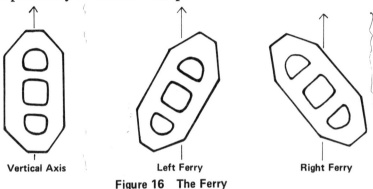

Vertical Axis   Left Ferry   Right Ferry

Figure 16   The Ferry

Once you have decided upon a course, note conspicuous hazards along the run for use as points of reference. Always plan an alternative course for each section of the rapids in the event that an error in maneuvering is made.

The Ferry

The term "ferry" simply means "to cross a river." In slow current, a boat may be ferried straight across the river, but in fast water, it is only possible to angle across. To avoid rocks and other obstacles in the river, it is necessary to constantly move the raft from one side of the river to the other. Generally, the rafter attempts to slow the raft's speed in the current, because the slower speed allows more time to move across the river and avoid hazards.

Assume there is a vertical axis and the raft is moving straight down the current of the river. The raft then moves off the vertical axis. The bow is to the right; the stern, to the left. This is a left ferry (because the position of the stern is to the left). Then the bow is to the left; the stern, to the right. This is a right ferry (because the position of the stern is to the right).

Imagine again that the raft is straight along the vertical axis. The raft may move ninety degrees either way before it is sideways to the current. Ordinarily, the best angle of the raft is forty-five degrees, either way, in relation to the river current.

To move across the river quickly, increase the angle of the raft relative to the current so the raft is on the ninety degree plane, at a right angle to the current. This increased angle position, however, will also increase the raft's speed downstream because there is more surface area to be moved by the current.

To slow the downstream speed of the raft, decrease the angle of the raft so it is along the vertical axis, or parallel to the current. (Downstream speed is slower because the surface area of the raft in the current is reduced.) This decreased angle position, however, will not allow movement of the raft across the river.

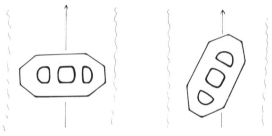

Increasing Angle
- o Permits movement across the river
- o Increases downstream speed

Decreasing Angle
- o Slows downstream speed
- o Prohibits movement across the river

Figure 17   Changing the Ferry Angle

The ferry position, therefore, allows the rafter to avoid river hazards by slowing the raft's downstream speed as it moves across the river. Odd as it may seem, the bow of the raft is pointed toward the obstacle to be avoided. Then the rafter rows or paddles against the current in order to slow the movement of the raft downstream. Suppose, for example, that the obstacle lies on the left side of the river. Generally, use the right ferry (stern to the right, bow to the left) so the raft can be rowed or paddled against the current. If the obstacle is on the right, use a left ferry (stern to the left, bow to the right) to allow rowing or paddling away from the hazard. If correctly used, the ferry will allow the raft to glide across the river as it moves downstream, missing the obstacle.

When running rapids, begin to ferry early enough to allow movement across the river in time to avoid obstacles. Minimize maneuvering as much as possible in large rapids. Keep the bow of the raft into the waves for the greatest stability. This is because a raft that is even slightly sideways in large rapids faces the possibility of overturning.

Rowing

The traditional rowing stroke involves a pulling motion of the oars. On calm water, the rower's back will be turned downstream while rowing, which requires occasional glancing over the shoulder to see ahead. This position is fine for still water but is awkward in fast water where there is a need to keep an eye on obstacles down river.

Early river runners followed the traditional method for years without question. Then in 1896 a man named Nathaniel Galloway decided to do things differently—he turned his boat with the stern downstream and rowed against the current to slow his speed with oncoming obstacles.

Pulling on the oars while facing downstream offers several advantages. First, it allows increased visibility of the rapids and other obstructions. Second, this pulling stroke is a strong stroke, because it uses body weight, the muscles of the back, and leg drive to power the stroke.

ROWING TECHNIQUE

The basic rowing technique will become instinctive after a little practice:

- Grab the handles of the oars and drop your wrists, causing the oars to lift from the water. Rock forward from the hips and simultaneously extend your arms. Keep the back fairly straight, head up, and eyes at a horizontal level. The blades of the oars should be no higher than necessary to clear the surface of the water.

- Straighten the wrists and relax the downward pressure of the hand on the handles to allow the blades to drop into the water.

- Now, the power of the stroke begins as the body moves from the forward to the vertical position. At the same time, extra power is generated by driving with the legs. The back and arms remain straight with the head level, as the trunk of the body goes into the layback position. When the arms finish

56

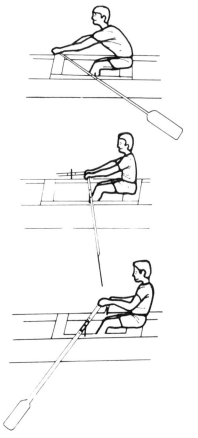

Rock forward from the hips and extend the arms. Keep the back of the body straight and the head level. Drop the blades in the water.

Take solid and deep strokes, dipping the oar blades to the throat. Apply power smoothly and steadily, rather than suddenly.

Let the arms finish the pull by pulling toward the chest. Allow the blades to glide out of the water to finish the stroke.

Figure 18   The Pulling Stroke

the pull, the elbows should be low as the hands come in toward the chest.

- At the end of the pull, a slight downward pressure on the handles will glide the blades from the water to finish the stroke. Then the trunk of the body swings forward from the hips as the hands are thrust forward, and the cycle is repeated.

On slow stretches of the river, alternate stroking can be especially effective. The momentum of the raft is gained during the pull stroke but diminishes when the oars are out of the water. A more uniform rate of speed can be maintained by stroking each oar alternately.

A pushing stroke may also be useful, in certain instances, either alone or to reinforce the basic pulling stroke. This stroke, however, is a weaker stroke than the pulling stroke, because it utilizes only the weaker muscles of the arms and abdomen. To execute the push stroke—lean back, place the forward oar blade in the water, and push with a straightened arm.

PIVOT STROKES

The raft will respond quickly to the single pulling stroke on one side of the raft. Pull on the right oar, the raft will move to the right. Pull on the left oar, the raft will move left.

Pulling on both of the oars at the same time will move the raft upstream in still water. In fast water it will slow the downstream speed of the raft.

In the calm water just above the rapids, it may be necessary to move ahead slightly without changing the bow-first position of the raft. A push stroke is helpful in this situation. Push on the right oar, the raft will move left. Push on the left oar, the raft will move right.

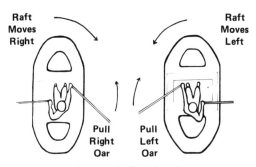

Figure 19 Pull Stroke

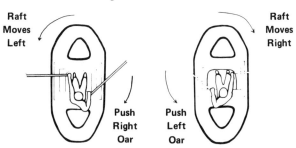

Figure 20 Push Stroke

DOUBLE OAR TURN

Pull on an oar and the raft will move in that direction. Push on an oar and the raft will move in the opposite direction. These basic pivot strokes are fine when used separately, but combining them gives added strength and speed. These combined strokes, known as the double oar turn, allow the raft to be moved easily and without any backward motion.

To move the raft to the right, pull on the right oar and push on the left. To move left, pull on the left oar and push on the right.

It takes a little practice but eventually this maneuver will become second nature. This stroke is especially helpful in turning the raft into the correct position before approaching the rapids. It is also useful to keep the bow of the raft directed straight into the waves of the rapids. This prevents the raft from moving sideways into the rapids and possibly flipping.

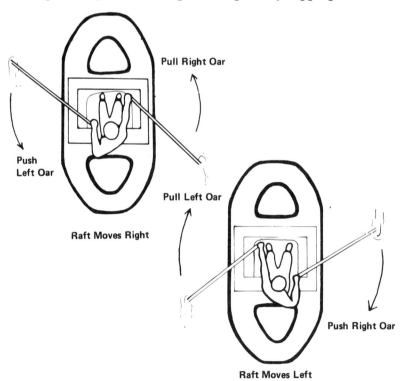

Pull Right Oar

Push Left Oar

Raft Moves Right

Pull Left Oar

Push Right Oar

Raft Moves Left

Figure 21   Right Double Oar Turn   Figure 22   Left Double Oar Turn

ROWING FERRY

The primary method of avoiding hazards in the river is to slow the raft's speed in the current and move across the river, averting a collision with the hazard. This ferry position, however, should be initiated early enough to allow the necessary movement for evading large rocks and reversals in the river. If a particular obstacle is to be avoided, the bow of the raft should be pointed toward that obstacle, and the rafter rows against the current to slow the speed of the raft downstream and move it across the river. Usually, the best angle is about forty-five degrees in relation to the current. A larger angle allows quicker movement across the river, but also increases downstream speed of the raft. Decreasing the angle slows downstream speed, but prevents movement across the width of the river.

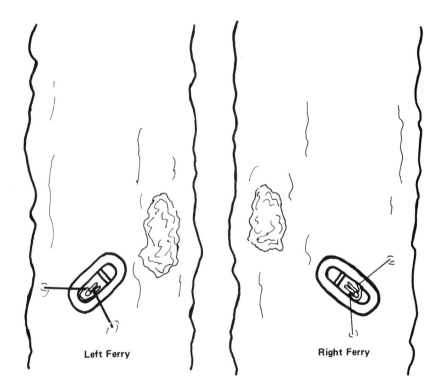

Left Ferry   Right Ferry

Figure 23   Rowing Ferry

BACK PIVOT

Ordinarily the raft floats downstream bow-first in either a right or left ferry position. There is usually sufficient room to change the ferry position and move to the other side of the river. In some instances, however, there is neither time nor space to change from one extreme ferry position to another. The back pivot is the stroke for this situation.

The back pivot consists of turning the raft from a ferry position to a stern-downstream position, thus allowing the raft to slip closely between the rocks. Due to the close proximity of the rocks, it may be difficult to maneuver the downstream oar. If so, it becomes necessary to pull frantically on the upstream oar in order to move the raft into the correct position. Because this stroke leaves the raft running backward, it should be used only rarely when a forward position is impossible.

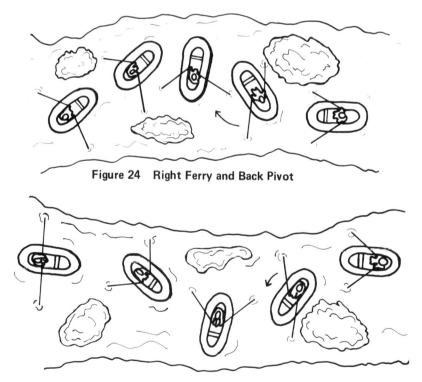

Figure 24   Right Ferry and Back Pivot

Figure 25   Left Ferry and Back Pivot

Paddling

Paddle rafts have become very popular in recent years, primarily because they allow greater participation among a tight-knit crew. A raft with oars generally responds more readily than a paddle-powered raft. This is because oars can be back stroked more strongly than paddles can, largely as a result of leverage. But a team of well experienced paddlers can negotiate almost any level of whitewater, and intermediate paddlers can easily tackle medium volume rivers. Paddle rafts, in fact, may even become a necessity on rivers that are too tight and rocky for oars.

PADDLING TECHNIQUE

Forward Stroke. The forward stroke is the basic and most commonly used stroke in river running for both forward motion and turning the raft. The stroke is made close to the side of the raft, with the paddle shaft moving on a vertical or near-vertical plane.

Grasp the grip of the paddle with one hand. With the other hand, grasp the shaft several inches above the paddle blade. To begin the stroke, lean forward, extending the lower arm full length and bending the upper arm at the elbow. Insert the blade into the water as far forward as is comfortable. Place the blade fairly close to the raft and dip the blade almost completely into the water. The lower arm pulls directly backward, and the upper arm drives forward at eye level.

The lower arm pulls backward until the hand is near the hip. At this point, both arms are relaxed, with the upper arm dropping down. This action causes the blade to rise to the surface of the water, and the blade is then swept above the surface of the water to repeat the cycle. This recovery back to the starting position should be made as close to the water as quickly as possible.

Avoid needless body motion in executing the forward stroke, for only a slight rotation of the body and shoulders should accompany the arm motion. Elimination of unnecessary body motion will allow greater smoothness and efficiency in the stroke.

62

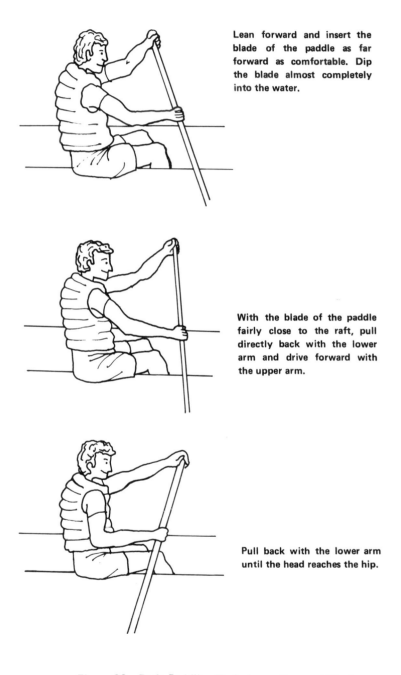

Lean forward and insert the
blade of the paddle as far
forward as comfortable. Dip
the blade almost completely
into the water.

With the blade of the paddle
fairly close to the raft, pull
directly back with the lower
arm and drive forward with
the upper arm.

Pull back with the lower arm
until the head reaches the hip.

Figure 26   Basic Paddling Technique—Forward Stroke

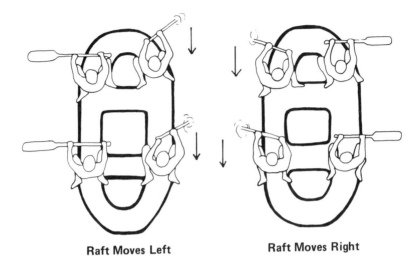

Raft Moves Left   Raft Moves Right

Figure 27   Left and Right Forward Stroke

Back Stroke. The movements of the back stroke are basically the reverse of those used in the forward stroke. They begin where the forward stroke ends. The bottom arm pushes down and forward while the upper arm pulls up and back. At the beginning of the stroke, the body leans somewhat forward and at the end of the stroke, should lean somewhat backward. The this stroke is derived from the use of the abdominal muscles and the muscles of the arms and shoulders, but it remains necessary to preserve a steady, erect body position.

In still water the back stroke will move the raft upstream. In fast water it is especially effective because it will slow the downstream speed of the raft while allowing good visibility of the obstacles down river.

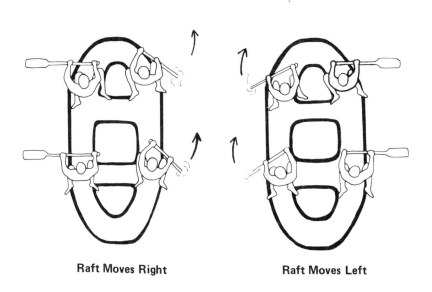

Raft Moves Right   Raft Moves Left

Figure 28   Back Stroke

PIVOT STROKES

To turn the raft, it is necessary to learn the basic pivot strokes. If the paddlers on the right side of the raft use the forward stroke, the raft moves left. If the left side uses the forward stroke, the raft moves right.

The back stroke is just the opposite and moves the raft in the same direction as the side on which it is used. Therefore, the back stroke on the right side moves the raft to the right. A back stroke on the left side moves the raft left.

DOUBLE PADDLE TURN

Although either a single forward stroke or a single back stroke will turn the raft, the turn can be quickened by combining these two basic pivot strokes.

To move the raft to the right, use a back stroke on the right side of the raft and a forward stroke on the left. To move the raft to the left, use a back stroke on the left side of the raft and a forward stroke on the right.

To negotiate these turns, the entire crew must be able to respond to a captain's commands of "Turn right" or "Turn left," with each paddler instinctively using the appropriate forward or back stroke.

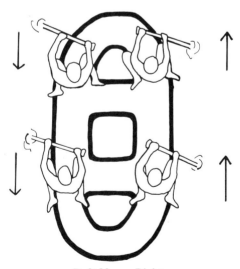

Raft Moves Right

Figure 29   **Right Double Paddle Turn**

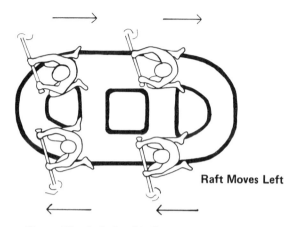

Raft Moves Left

Figure 30   Left Double Paddle Turn

Photo courtesy of Campways

SIDEWAYS STROKES

On tight, rocky rivers it may be necessary to move the raft sideways, in addition to the usual turning maneuvers. In this case, use the draw stroke, which is a sideways pull of the paddle toward the raft. The draw stroke starts by placing the blade parallel to the paddler as far as is comfortable, then drawing the paddle in toward the paddler. It is especially important to grasp the shaft of the paddle firmly with the lower hand and to pull the blade steadily toward the boat. To move the raft sideways to the right, use a draw stroke on the right. To move the raft sideways to the left, use a draw stroke on the left.

The opposite of the draw stroke is the pry stroke, which is a sideways push of the paddle away from the raft. Start the pry stroke with the paddle blade near the side of the raft and with your upper arm over the water. Exert the push with your lower arm while pulling the upper arm in toward you.

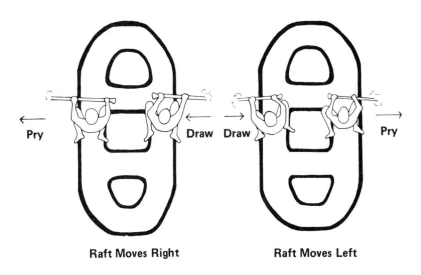

Figure 31   Sideways Stroke

Combining a draw stroke and a pry stroke allows the raft to be moved sideways quickly, and these strokes are especially effective with the smaller rafts in the 12 to 13 foot range.

The basic commands are simply, "Draw right" (with left pry) and "Draw left" (with right pry).

STERN MANEUVERS

A paddler at the stern can add greatly to the maneuverability of the raft. The most common function of this position is simply as a rudder—angle the paddle blade to the right side for a right turn and angle the blade to the left side for a left turn. Other strokes at the stern, such as a forward stroke or draw stroke, will also allow the raft to turn faster. An abrupt forward stroke or pry stroke on one side of the raft will cause the raft to move in the opposite direction.

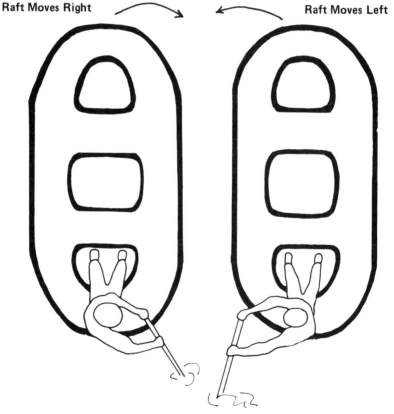

Raft Moves Right   Raft Moves Left

Figure 32   Using Rudder at the Stern

PADDLING FERRY

To avoid rocks and other obstacles in the river, it is necessary to constantly move the raft from one side of the river to the other. This movement is known as "ferrying." By paddling upstream, the paddlers can effectively slow the raft's speed in the current. But to use the more powerful forward stroke, the bow of the raft and the paddlers must face upstream, requiring the paddlers to look over their shoulders to see the rapids ahead.

If the bow remains downstream, the paddlers can keep an eye on the obstacles down river. To slow the raft's speed, however, the paddlers must use a back stroke, which is a fairly weak stroke in fast water.

Because the forward stroke provides poor visibility downstream and the back stroke is relatively weak, a paddle raft requires more advance planning in running rapids than a rowed raft which responds more quickly.

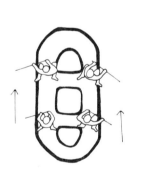 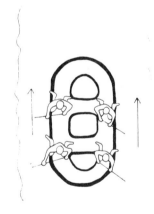

Bow Downstream
- o Good visibility
- o Weaker back stroke

Bow Upstream
- o Stronger forward stroke
- o Poor visibility

Figure 33 The Paddle Ferry

4

River Camping

Most rafters regard overnight camping as a valuable and unforgettable part of their river experience. The general increase in outdoor recreation has led to the development and improvement of camping equipment, much of which is well suited for use on the river. In addition to a knowledge of equipment, river camping involves an understanding of campsite selection and sanitation. Both of these are necessary to ensure the safety and health of the campers and to prevent damage to the natural environment.

Clothing and Personal Gear

The clothing and personal gear necessary on a river trip depend on the climate and length of the trip undertaken. Comfort, durability, and ease of care are primary factors in the selection of clothes, while personal gear is largely dependent upon the preferences of the individual.

CLOTHING

Pack as lightly as possible. To greatly reduce the number of clothes needed on a trip, wash them every other day. These clothes can be dried in camp during the evening or on the raft during the day. Always have a set of dry clothes to change into at the end of the day.

Most rafters prefer to wear shorts during the day on warm weather trips. The warm weather will dry your clothes after you have been drenched in the rapids. A wide brimmed hat will help prevent sunburn, and a wet bandana tied around the neck will keep you cool.

71

In cold weather, or where the river temperature is cold (or where there are continuous rapids that keep you constantly wet), most prefer to wear either a rain parka and pants or a nylon windbreaker. A more specialized version of these windbreakers is well known to kayakers as paddle jackets. Made of heavy waterproof nylon with tight-fitting closures around the wrists and neck, these paddle jackets are well suited for rafting. These jackets should be tied to the duffle for the chance of rain or the coolness of the afternoon before unpacking the gear.

Both windbreakers and paddle jackets are especially warm when worn with an insulating layer of wool. But for colder temperatures, either air or water, a wet suit provides the greatest amount of protection. When prolonged exposure to colder temperatures is possible, a wet suit is necessary not only for comfort but for safety.

Tennis shoes are the best shoes to wear on the raft. They dry out easily and the corrugated soles provide good traction on rocks for scouting rapids or hiking. If a rafter falls into the river, tennis shoes are necessary protection for fending off rocks while floating downstream.

Gloves for rowing or paddling are helpful to prevent blisters and provide warmth. For the cold weather rafter, a device similar to a glove, known as a "pogie," is best. The pogie, made of waterproof nylon, encloses the hand and the handle of the oar or paddle, yet does not come between the handle and the hand. Pogies are ideal for retaining heat and repelling wind and water, but at the same time, they allow direct contact with the oar or paddle handle.

Clothes often become wet, so it is best to choose fabrics that dry quickly. Most natural fibers absorb water easily, so it is best to wear clothes that contain a blend of natural and synthetic fibers. The blends are both comfortable and quick-drying. A blend of cotton and polyester is a perfect combination for river trips, but heavy denim materials, especially slow in drying, should be avoided. Underwear, too, can cause chafing when wet, and synthetics, such as nylon (a lightweight bathing suit works well), are better suited for use on the river. For cold weather trips, wool is a necessity. Wool's ability to retain heat even when wet is its primary advantage.

Rain and wind parkas are usually made of nylon, either coated or uncoated. Uncoated nylon fabrics provide good protection but are not water repellent for extended periods. They should not be used for rain protection. Coated fabrics, on the other hand, afford a greater measure of water repellency, but condensation inside a garment made from a coated fabric must be expected. Coated fabrics cannot be considered completely waterproof because any seam is vulnerable to moisture and should be treated with a seam sealer.

The newest developments in fabrics are fabric laminates consisting of a microporous polymeric film with a fabric bonded to one or both sides. This material provides water repellency and breathability. The fabric protects the film from water and abrasion, and the film keeps out water but allows water vapor to pass through. Laboratory tests have proven these fabrics more waterproof than urethane-coated nylon and yet more permeable to water vapor than cotton/polyester poplin. These fabrics are expensive, but further developments and mass-production should lead to a price reduction.

PERSONAL GEAR

In addition to clothing, rafters inevitably include a variety of personal gear to suit their individual needs and interests.

Lights. Modern camping lanterns are commonly powered by white gasoline, butane/propane, or a 6-volt battery. These lanterns provide a great deal of light (especially lights with fluorescent bulbs) for activity around the camp. Several models are available, and the amount of light emitted, as well as the burning time, vary from model to model. Most liquid fuel lanterns contain glass globes and necessitate either a carrying case or protective padding to prevent breakage of the globe.

A more traditional source of light is the candle lantern. Candle lanterns are durable, inexpensive, lightweight, and add a pleasant glow to a campsite. The simplest model consists of a light metal case with a glass chimney, while another model folds flat in storage, then springs open for use. A more sophisticated model is cylindrical in shape and telescopes open for use. The candle flame in this model remains in the same position at all times because a spring in the holder keeps moving the candle up as it burns.

Once you have decided upon a candle lantern, you will need candles. If possible, use stearine candles or those with a high stearic acid content (preferably forty-five percent or more). These candles have a higher than normal melting point, allowing them to drip less and burn longer than ordinary plumber's candles. When trying to decide how many candles to take on a trip, remember most four-inch stearic acid candles are rated to burn about three hours.

For a more directional light, most campers pack a conventional flashlight. Several models and sizes are available, but select a durable one. Flashlights vary according to the size of the battery used. A larger battery, or a third battery, provides a stronger beam and longer life. The standard (carbon zinc) flashlight battery is entirely adequate for intermittent use. If, however, the flashlight has to be left on for long periods, the standard battery quickly loses energy and its light soon dims to a useless glow. An alkaline battery is far more efficient and, under continuous use, will provide at least five times the life of the standard battery. Alkaline batteries also function more effectively in extreme temperatures (especially below freezing) than standard batteries. These advantages of the alkaline battery would seem to outweigh the disadvantages of higher cost and weight.

Regardless of the lantern or flashlight used, carry extra fuel, batteries, mantles, or light bulbs.

Day pack. A day pack is useful for short side hikes during the day. Because the pack is small and lightweight, it can be easily stored when not in use. Choose a sturdy model made of nylon or canvas.

Canteens. A couple of plastic, quart-size water bottles should be included with the rest of the personal gear. These water bottles are necessary for side hikes, especially in hot climates.

Knives. Knives are not as indispensable as it is commonly assumed. They are occasionally useful for cutting rope or nylon cord, and they can be handy in cleaning fish. A sheath knife, while more convenient, is bulkier than a folding knife.

Soap. When bathing or washing your hands, use only biodegradable soaps and shampoos.

Toothpaste and toothbrushing. Biodegradable soaps suitable for brushing teeth are now available. To brush teeth using ordinary toothpaste, use a bowl filled with water as a basin, and after brushing, dump the water at least 100 feet away from the high water line of the river.

Other gear. Other personal gear may be necessary for a more comfortable trip. Sunglasses, suntan lotion, lip balm and mosquito repellent are commonly included. Individual interests will dictate other gear such as camera, hiking boots, fishing equipment, or binoculars.

Sleeping Gear and Tents

To assure a good night's sleep, the rafter must choose the proper sleeping bag and pad, and possibly some type of tarp or tent as shelter. Advancements in design, materials, and manufacturing techniques have improved the quality of these products. These advancements have also complicated the decision of which model to purchase.

SLEEPING BAGS

The purpose of a sleeping bag is the efficient prevention of body heat loss in order to maintain a constant body temperature under varying temperature and wind conditions. During sleep, several factors contribute to this loss of body heat:

- *Ground temperature.* The sleeping bag compresses under a person's weight and exposes the body to the cold ground.
- *Wind.* Moving wind at the surface of the sleeping bag not only conducts heat away from the bag but actually penetrates the bag to some extent.
- *Metabolism.* Individuals differ greatly in their rates of metabolism, which in turn affects the body's production of heat and its need for additional insulation.
- *Other factors.* Relative humidity, altitude, and even the individual's emotional state will influence the need for warmth.

To minimize body heat loss, a sleeping bag employs insulating materials of different types. Dead air space, created by the insulation within the sleeping bag, provides most of the warmth. The shell and lining of the bag also retain heat by curbing the radiation of heat away from the body. Any material that prevents air from circulating within the layers of the sleeping bag will provide effective insulation. Therefore, the degree of warmth provided does not depend on the type of material used but on its thickness.

Because the insulating material determines a sleeping bag's weight and bulk, this material must be capable of compressing into a small space for packing while returning to its original thickness when released. At the same time, it must provide the greatest insulation thickness for its weight. Goose down or duck down remains more lightweight, compressible, and resilient than synthetic fills, but it is also more expensive. In addition to cost, synthetic fills have another important advantage over down. That is, when down becomes wet, it is useless, but synthetic fills retain their loft even when wet (and they also dry more quickly than down). Although a well-sealed waterproof bag will protect the sleeping bag from the spray of the rapids, any bag may become wet in a rainy or humid climate.

The designs of sleeping bags are generally classified into two categories: semi-rectangular and mummy. The semi-rectangular shape is roomier than the mummy and is fine for three-season use, but the mummy remains the best design for cold weather use because its slim fit and head coverage provide maximum thermal efficiency.

The construction of the sleeping bag is another important consideration in the selection of a particular model. The bag is divided into a series of self-contained tubes that prevent the fill from shifting to the bottom of the sleeping bag and away from the areas of greatest wear. The stitching of the tubes has a definite effect upon the efficiency of the sleeping bag, for these seams may permit the exposure of cold spots in the bag.

A sewn-through construction, which is simply an inner and outer shell stitched together, is the least expensive method. While it is suitable for warm weather sleeping bags, it is not suitable for bags designed for cold weather use. In synthetic-filled bags, two sewn-through quilts may be arranged so that the seams are alternated to eliminate cold spots. In down bags, a widely used method is the box construction, in which a vertical baffle forms a wall between inner and outer shells for a more uniform thickness. Similar to the box construction, but more effective, is the slant-tube construction. In this construction, a longer, sloping baffle creates an overlapping tube effect. The most effective system for retaining a uniform distribution of down, however, is the overlapping V-tube construction, consisting of small triangular compartments that interlock and limit the expansion of the tubes.

Several other features are present on most well-made sleeping bags. A zipper baffle (or draft tube) prohibits wind and cold air from entering the bag at the zipper. It also prevents the body from coming in contact with the cold zipper. A two-way zipper allows for better ventilation in warmer temperatures. The more expensive down mummy bags include a channel block baffle and differential cut. The channel block baffle is a baffle between the inner and outer shell, extending the length of the side seam, that prevents down from shifting from the top to the bottom of the bag. A bag with a differential cut features an outer shell larger than the inner shell in order to eliminate cold spots.

It is advisable to purchase the bag from a reliable manufacturer because the contents and manufacturing techniques of the sleeping bag are concealed from the view of the consumer.

SLEEPING PADS

Sleeping pads serve primarily to provide comfort while sleeping, but they also furnish insulation for the sleeping bag against the cool ground. Several types of sleeping pads are now available—air mattresses, foam pads, and a recent development combining air and foam.

Air Mattresses. Air mattresses are by far the most comfortable form of sleeping pad. They fold up to a small space when not being used, and inflate in a minute or two. But air mattresses are not perfect. They are not suited for temperatures below freezing, and can develop leaks that are difficult to repair.

Air mattresses can be made of thin vinyl or tough, vulcanized rubber. The cheap vinyl mattresses tear easily, and the seams are often weak. Mattresses made of vulcanized rubber are the sturdiest, but they are also the heaviest. The middle and most popular mattresses are those made of coated nylon with multiple, separate chambers (usually six to nine chambers). Several models use a ripstop nylon cover with compartments into which removable vinyl tubes slip.

Foam pads. Foam pads have become very popular in recent years. Although bulkier and not quite as expensive as air mattresses, they are extremely durable and provide excellent insulation qualities. Foam pads can generally be classified into two categories: closed cell and open cell.

Closed cell pads are usually made from a type of polyethylene foam that will not absorb water. The most popular closed cell pad, known as Ensolite, compresses very little and insulates well, making it ideal for winter use. Another closed cell pad is marketed under the name of Volarfoam. Volarfoam is about half the weight of Ensolite, but it is less resilient and breaks more easily.

These closed cell foams such as Ensolite and Volarfoam are usually available in thicknesses of ¼-inch, 3/8-inch, and ½-inch. The 3/8-inch seems a good compromise between insulation (it is effective to 5 degrees) and comfort and weight and bulk.

Open cell foam pads, made of a type of polyurethane, have become the most popular sleeping pad. These pads provide greater comfort than closed cell foam, but they require about three times the thickness for equivalent insulation (a 2-inch pad is effective to about minus 10 degrees). Since an open cell pad will absorb water, most include a fabric covering. This cover is ordinarily made with cotton/polyester on top to prevent the sleeping bag from slipping off and to allow the evaporation of moisture. The bottom is usually a tough, coated nylon. These covers often contain nylon tie straps and a built-in pillow section.

One model combines the advantageous qualities of open and closed cell foam by bonding a ¼-inch closed cell sheet to a 1¼-inch open cell sheet. The result is a pad that combines zero-degree warmth with the comfort and resilience of open cell foam, all at a negligible increase in weight.

Combination of air and foam. Another model consists of an open cell foam pad inserted inside a nylon air mattress—thus combining the insulation of open cell foam and the cushioning of an air mattress. This mattress unrolls and self-inflates when the valve is open. For stowing, open the valve, unroll the mattress, then reclose the valve.

BIVOUAC COVERS

One alternative to a groundsheet and tarp, and perhaps even a tent, is the bivouac cover (or bivouac "bag"). The bivouac cover is actually a rectangular nylon envelope into which a sleeping bag slips. Completely covering the sleeping bag, the bivouac cover offers several advantages by:

- Replacing the groundsheet and tarp
- Warding off wind and light rain
- Reducing abrasion and soiling of the sleeping bag shell
- Increasing insulation (the dead air space will add about 10 degrees effectiveness to sleeping bag warmth)
- Preventing the sleeping pad from slipping beneath the sleeping bag

Most models incorporate a breathable nylon top and a waterproof-coated nylon bottom. A zipper inserted along half the length of the bivouac cover permits easy entry and exit. Grommets are often provided to allow the cover to be staked down.

TENTS

The simplest form of tent is a tarp, typically made of nylon or polyethylene with metal grommets attached along the edges. A more sophisticated version of the tarp incorporates additional "D" rings and nylon webbing, allowing the tarp tent to be pitched in an endless number of combinations. For even more versatility, use commercially manufactured tabs that attach to any portion of the tarp and provide additional lashing points.

The tube tent is slightly more advanced than the tarp. Made of plastic (or sometimes nylon), these tube tents are inexpensive and provide adequate shelter in milder conditions. Both tarps and tube tents can be pitched between properly spaced trees, but tent poles, pegs and guy lines should be packed in the event that adequate trees are not present.

For the most complete protection from rain, wind, and insects, conventional tents are the best shelter. The tent should be durable, lightweight, and compact when stored, in addition to being waterproof. Cotton canvas tents were widely used for many years but have largely been replaced by nylon models.

Canvas is extremely durable and resistant to abrasion but it is heavy and will mildew when wet.

Most campers prefer nylon because of its light weight, strength, compactness, resistance to mildew, and ease of maintenance. Tents constructed of a single wall of waterproof, coated fabric are hot, and because of the cooler temperature outside the tent (especially at night or during rainy weather), body moisture will condense on the tent's inner walls and drip to the floor of the tent. As a result of this condensation, most tents include an uncoated nylon tent with a coated nylon fly sheet suspended over the tent. The condensed water passes through the inner tent and condenses on the inside of the fly sheet. To keep condensed water from contacting the inner tent, the fly sheet should be pitched tightly with several inches remaining between the tent and the sheet. The fly sheet should be long enough to touch the ground on each side of the tent in order to prevent the sheet from whipping in the wind and to provide greater wind and water protection.

Tents are available in a variety of structural designs, ranging from the A-frame to sophisticated geometric shapes and frame systems. The A-frame tent is the most popular. These tents contain aluminum poles set at an angle and joined at the ridge of the tent. They are light and relatively easy to set up, and if correctly pitched, their low profile provides superior stability in high winds. Other designs, including free-standing and dome tents, are roomy, and the fiberglass poles allow easy set up. These tents will remain stable if staked down securely.

The design of a tent is actually more important than the techniques used in its manufacture (number of stitches per inch and the like). Most well designed tents feature a "catenary cut." That means the tent's side panels are cut in curves that will, when the tensions of the erected tent are applied, compensate as accurately as possible for the tent's tendency to sag. The tent, therefore, remains taut and does not collect water or flap unduly in the wind (which is the key to stability). A well designed tent is simply more durable in rough usage than a well sewn but poorly designed tent, so it pays to check around and buy from an established and reliable manufacturer.

Several other features distinguish a good quality tent. A "bathtub" or wrap-up floor that extends several inches on the sides of the tent eliminates seams on the ground and provides better waterproofing. Nylon coil zippers are superior to those made of metal, and mosquito-netted rear windows allow cross-ventilation on warm nights. Shock cord running inside the tent poles allows faster set up and prevents the loss of poles. Some tents even include lantern loops, clothesline rings, or small interior pockets for limited storage.

After purchasing a new tent, thoroughly waterproof all its seams. Attach shock cord to all guy lines to reduce the stress on the seams of the tent in heavy winds or rain. In high winds and extended storms, an A-frame tent should be pitched with one end facing the prevailing gale to reduce the tent's resistance to the wind. In warm weather tents should be pitched with the open entrance facing the wind in order to prevent flapping. If the closed end faces the wind, pressure differences will cause incessant flapping. During storms or cold weather where the tent must be securely closed, some flapping is inevitable.

The Kitchen

Rafting has a way of building an appetite. The food that can be packed for a river trip ranges widely and depends on individual tastes and the amount of space available. Water is also essential and usually requires purification. Methods of cooking and cookware, as well as dishwashing techniques, must all be considered in order to ensure a safe and efficient kitchen.

FOOD

When choosing what foods to take, consider several factors:

- Nutrition
- Weight
- Ease of preparation
- Taste
- Cost

It is possible to keep the cooking simple and still produce a palatable and nourishing meal. The nutrition requirements of the individuals on the trip are of prime concern. From 3,000 to 4,000 calories per day are required for an active person on a vigorous raft trip. Eat foods from each of the four food groups and drink plenty of water to maintain a balanced intake. Strenuous activity causes increased perspiration and the attendant loss of salt, requiring additional salting of food to replace that which is lost.

On trips lasting only a couple of days, it is not as crucial to reduce the weight and bulk of food as it is on extended trips. Fresh meats, fruits, and vegetables can be carried in ice chests for the first several days, with special care taken to detect spoilage (include a thermometer inside the ice chest to ensure that the temperature is at least 45 degrees F.). On shorter trips, all food can be canned goods, but on longer trips some of these cans will usually be replaced by dehydrated and freeze-dried foods to reduce the weight and bulk. (Remember that an overloaded raft presents a serious safety problem.) Fortunately, modern methods of food processing have produced a vast number of excellent quick-cooking products that are lightweight, compact, and readily available. These foods can be stored for months without refrigeration and, if unopened, will not spoil. Many are pre-cooked and ready to serve after boiling water is added, while others require a minimal amount of cooking.

Dehydrated foods are processed by moving through ovens that extract 80 percent to 97 percent of the food's moisture, shrinking it, and significantly reducing its weight. Many dehydrated foods are readily available in grocery stores and are less expensive than their freeze-dried counterparts.

Freeze-dried foods are frozen in vacuum chambers at temperatures as low as minus 50 degrees F. The solid ice in the food is changed directly into a gas vapor that is wicked away in the chamber, leaving the food literally freeze-dried. This process preserves the original color, nutritional value, and shape of the food, leaving it in a very porous state for quick rehydration. These freeze-dried foods are extremely lightweight and are available from most outdoor equipment shops and catalogs.

Menus must take individual tastes into account, so it is best to have all members participate in menu planning.

Breakfast. Breakfast usually consists of the typical bacon and eggs, toast and pancakes (try adding walnuts or cinnamon to the pancake batter). Other suggested breakfast items include instant oatmeal or cream of wheat, stewed fruits, breakfast

meats, hash brown potatoes, and biscuits with honey or preserves. Other "instant" breakfast foods, requiring little or no
preparation, are available from the grocery store. Coffee, hot
tea or chocolate, and other breakfast drinks may also be offered.

Lunch. A quick, energizing lunch, requiring no cooking and
little preparation, is best, because the middle of the day is occu-
pied with activity. Lunch might include sandwiches (use dense,
whole-grained bread that does not crush as easily), dried sau-
sage or beef jerky, fruits, nuts, crackers and cheese, granola
bars, and candy.

Snacks. Dried fruits, raisins, hard candies and a mixture of
nuts, raisins, and chocolate chips (commonly known as "gorp")
make excellent snacks.

Supper. The evening meal is ordinarily the largest meal of the
day. Soups are easy to prepare and are usually served as the
first course of the meal. The main course can be chosen from a
wide variety of fresh, dehydrated or freeze-dried meats, fruits,
and vegetables. Several easy-to-prepare mixes are available in
the grocery store, including skillet dinners, macaroni and
cheese dinners, flavored rice, and mashed potatoes. Puddings or
cobblers can be served as dessert.

Spices. Because the rafter is somewhat confined to the type of
foods and cooking methods used, spices are the key for providing taste to otherwise routine and bland meals (especially dehydrated and freeze-dried dinners). A number of spices may be
added to enrich the taste of food:

- Apple pie spice: Can be used in apple cobblers, sweet potatoes, squash, French toast, and puddings.
- Anise seed: Use when preparing baked apples, fruit salads,
  stewed fruits, or baked fish.
- Barbecue sauce: A blend of spices with a slightly "smoked"
  flavor. Use when preparing beef, pork, baked beans, peas,
  potatoes, chicken, or fish.
- Beef flavor base and chicken seasoned stock base: two all-
  purpose seasonings. Adds a rich flavor to soups, stews, gravies, vegetables, rice, noodles, and casseroles. Can also be
  used to make stock or broth.

- Bell pepper flakes: Adds flavor to vegetable soup, clam chowder, stews, chicken casseroles, and Spanish rice.
- Cinnamon sugar: A perfect blend of ground cinnamon and sugar used in making cinnamon toast. Use to sprinkle over baked apples, stewed fruit, French toast, pancakes, or waffles.
- Cumin: Use whole or ground in hamburgers, stews, lentil soup, pea soup, rice, dried bean dishes, or potato salad.
- Dill seed: Use when preparing cabbage, sauerkraut, green beans, or fish. Dill salt, a blend of ground dill seed and salt, can be used on tomatoes, potatoes, and tossed green salads.
- Garlic: Use in preparing tossed green salads, beef, lamb, pork, veal, variety meats, green beans, tomatoes, tomato sauce, spaghetti sauce, broiled and baked fish, and bread.
- Meat tenderizer: Available seasoned and non-seasoned. Use to tenderize less tender cuts of meat such as chuck, round steak, stew meat, brisket, or flank steak.

- Onion: A versatile product in many forms. Use in dishes where an onion flavor is desired. Onion juice can be used in dishes where a mild onion flavor is desired without the particles of onion.
- Pepper: The universal seasoning. Use when preparing meats, vegetables, soups, and salads.
- Tarragon: An excellent herb to use when preparing fish. Use when preparing chicken and tossed green salads.
- Vegetable flakes: A blend of dehydrated vegetables. Use in stew, soups, gravies, and casseroles.

Packing food. To eliminate confusion, the food should be packed in an orderly manner. Sort the food either according to the meal (all breakfast items together, all lunch items together, and so forth) or by the day, and mark the containers accordingly. Remove all unnecessary cardboard and paper wrappers to eliminate as much weight and bulk as possible. Flour, sugar, coffee, and drink mixes can be placed in plastic bags to reduce space as the contents are consumed. Dehydrated and freeze-dried foods can be placed in nylon stuff bags, while crushable items (especially eggs) should be packed in rigid plastic or light-weight aluminum containers. Plastic squeeze tubes are easy to store and can be used for honey, jam, peanut butter, and margarine.

WATER

Unfortunately, few rivers and streams in the country are safe for drinking without treatment of some sort. On short trips many rafters carry their own supply of water. But the weight (more than eight pounds per gallon) and bulk of water prohibit this practice on longer trips with larger numbers of passengers. Water purification, therefore, becomes a necessity. To purify water, as well as store it for cooking and drinking, water containers must be available.

Water purification. The oldest method of purifying water is simply to boil it for at least three minutes. This method is convenient for water used in cooking, since the water is usually boiled anyway.

Halazone tablets, a chlorine-releasing compound available at any drug store, are also widely used for the purification of water. Or, simply use undiluted chlorine bleach: Add eight drops of bleach to each gallon of water (double this amount if the water is cloudy). Mix thoroughly and let the water stand thirty minutes before drinking.

Iodine, as found in most first aid kits, is also capable of purifying water. Add four drops of iodine to each gallon of water (double this amount if the water is cloudy). Mix thoroughly and let the water stand for thirty minutes before drinking.

Other water purification chemicals and filtering devices are available and can be found in any outdoor equipment store or catalog.

Most of these purification methods will not leave a detectable taste if the water is allowed to stand for a sufficient time. If a slight aftertaste does persist, add a drink mix to the water to conceal this taste.

Water containers. The most inexpensive and lightweight water container is a collapsible, plastic container equipped with a handle and spigot. Once water is consumed and the container is empty, it may be folded to reduce its space. These containers are usually available in 2½- and 5-gallon sizes, but the 2½-gallon size is the most convenient because the weight of the 5-gallon container (more than forty pounds when full) is unhandy. More durable than these collapsible containers are those made of sturdy plastic, commonly known as Jerry cans.

For drinking during the day, a small beverage cooler with a spigot is ideal. The 1- and 2-gallon sizes, depending on the size of the party, are handy and allow the addition of drink mixes to the water.

A folding bucket made of coated fabric is very space efficient and can double as a wash basin for clothes (and yourself). Use biodegradable soap and ditch the water at least 100 feet from the river's high water level.

FIRES

Many river cooks prefer to use a wood or charcoal fire for cooking. In the case of wood fires, the kindling should include wood which burns quickly and easily. Pick up small branches and large twigs from the ground if they have not rotted; the bark from dead trees is also excellent kindling.

Hardwoods (such as oak, maple, hickory, ash, beech, and mesquite) are best for fuel because they burn down to long-lasting coals and produce little smoke. Look for driftwood or fallen branches that are so dry that you can bend them. Avoid wood that does a lot of popping and smoking or produces an odor when it burns (such as basswood, box elder, chestnut, sassafras, tulip, white elm, willow, or tamarack).

To produce the best coals for cooking, light the fire at least half an hour before you put the food on.

Firepans. A fire pan should always be used. The firepan helps contain the fire, along with the ashes and charcoal it produces, and reduces its scarring of the ground. A heavy gauge baking pan with a turned-up edge may be adequate for small fires, but large pans, usually made of sheet steel (such as the bottom of a 50-gallon metal barrel), are necessary for larger fires.

Be sure to mark the spot where the firepan was used so no one will walk through the area and burn their feet after the pan has been removed. The remaining ashes and charcoal from the firepan should always be containerized and carried out of the campsite for proper disposal.

Fire grills. Grills are commonly used in conjunction with the firepan. Most grills are lightweight and are constructed of nickel-plated, chrome-plated or stainless steel.

Fire starters. Some type of fire starter is necessary to ignite a campfire or camping stove. Most campers use ordinary matches to ignite their camping stoves. The common wood strike-any-where matches do not require a special surface for striking and even a wet surface will suffice if it is first partially dried. To ensure proper striking, matches must be kept dry in a water-proof match container. These containers are usually made of plastic or metal and sealed with a rubber gasket.

Water resistant safety matches will light even after they have been submerged in water for several minutes. These matches will absorb water, however, if they remain wet for long periods of time, rendering the matches impossible to light. Water resis-tant matches also require a special striking surface. It is impor-tant to keep this striking surface dry. Carry the striker and matches in a waterproof match container to keep them dry.

Many campers simply use disposable-type butane cigarette lighters to ignite their camping stoves. These lighters are not only convenient but are inexpensive. But be sure to carry a spare.

For starting campfires, there are a couple of other fire start-ing devices that are more reliable than matches. Several of these devices consist of metal strikers and flint striking pads. Others include a rod or block manufactured from magnesium or other space-age oxides. To use these fire starters, scrape off a small pile of shavings from the device with a pocket knife. The shav-ings should be bunched together into a compact pile and placed in a piece of tinder (a cupped piece of paper works well). Now, briskly scrape the device (or its sparking insert) to produce sparks directly into the shavings to ignite the tinder. Magnesi-um fire starters are especially effective, because they are capa-ble of producing a fire in wet weather or with damp tinder. Other starters require absolutely dry tinder.

If all the wood in the campsite area is wet, matches or fire starting devices alone will not start a fire. If this is the case, spread a flammable paste onto the wet wood. Once lit, the paste will burn for a long time. This flammable paste is also ideal for priming white gas and kerosene camping stoves.

CAMPING STOVES

Camping stoves provide two distinct advantages over camp-fires. They provide greater efficiency in cooking and they present less of a fire hazard. These stoves may be required in some areas, including many national parks and forests, where regulations prohibit open campfires.

Many lightweight camping stoves, designed for backpacking, are well suited for river work. Larger groups of rafters can either use a two-burner model or several of the smaller backpacking models. Although many excellent models of camping stoves are available, users of a particular model often become very attached to their stoves and remain staunch advocates of that model.

The most popular camping stoves are those that use white gasoline. White gas burns well, is easily obtainable, and is inexpensive. As a fuel white gas is very efficient by weight and burns cleanly so it will not soot pots and pans. It is also volatile enough so it is unnecessary to preheat the vaporizing tube between the fuel tank and the burner head. This volatility of gasoline, however, renders it potentially dangerous if it should explode.

Several features available for gasoline stoves are especially advantageous. A windscreen, for example, is helpful to maintain the flame and to increase the efficiency of the stove. A built-in cleaning needle also simplifies the job of keeping the flame orifice free of debris. For cold weather use, a small pressure pump is especially beneficial, and perhaps even a necessity, to maintain the pressure that keeps the fuel flowing through the vaporizing tube.

Butane and propane stoves are also popular. Their primary advantage is the convenience offered by the fuel which is packaged in a pressurized can, eliminating the need of filling, preheating, and priming the stove, as required with liquid fuel stoves. To use these butane and propane stoves simply turn them on and light.

Butane and propane stoves, however, are not perfect. These fuels are not as efficient as white gasoline, are more expensive, and are not as readily available. These stoves also operate so little heat is conducted from the stove to the fuel cartridge. The pressure in the cartridge decreases as the fuel is consumed, so it may take two to three times as long to boil water with an almost empty cartridge as with a new cartridge.

Cold weather use of a butane or propane stove is less efficient than a gasoline stove equipped with a pressure pump. However, at least one propane stove model preheats the gas before emission by wrapping the vaporizing tube around the burner, and this feature allows this model to operate more efficiently in cold weather than other butane and propane stoves.

Kerosene and alcohol stoves are also available although they are not widely used in this country. Kerosene is less volatile than gasoline and thus requires a more volatile priming fuel to preheat the vaporizing tube. A hand pump is necessary in order to ensure sufficient fuel tank pressure capable of maintaining a flame. Kerosene is also more accessible in Europe, Nepal, and Africa where white gas is difficult, or impossible, to obtain.

Alcohol, on the other hand, is a clean and convenient fuel, but it is very expensive in small quantities and does not produce as much heat as other fuel.

Priming the stove. Before lighting any gasoline stove, it must first be primed by preheating the vaporizing tube. First, fill the priming cup at the foot of the burner with gasoline or a flammable paste. Most campers who use white gas to prime the stove fill this priming cup with an eyedropper. If the stove is equipped with a pump, you can build up pressure and open the valve, releasing a small amount of fuel into the priming cup.

Now, light the gasoline or flammable paste in the priming cup, and this flame will heat the vaporizing tube. When the flame has almost finished burning, open the stove valve. If your timing is good, the dying flame from the priming cup will light the jet of the burner head. If the jet does not light, apply a match. The heat from the burner head will maintain the pressure in the fuel tank as long as the stove is operating.

To preheat a kerosene stove, simply spread flammable paste around the priming cup or on the vaporizing tube, then light. When the flame is almost extinguished, light the burner head.

Overheating of the stove. Butane and propane stoves are not prone to overheating because little heat is conducted from the stove to the fuel cartridge. Overheating can occur in a gasoline stove, most often the result of using cooking pots that are too large and hang over the fuel tank of the stove. The surface of the pot reflects heat back to the tank and causes the overheating. Avoid this situation by using smaller pots or by purchasing a larger stove.

If the stove exceeds its ability to vent this high heat and pressure, the safety valve in the tank filler cap will give way in order to release this overpressure. The flammable gas vapor is then released through the filler cap and will ignite into a shooting, pulsating flame. If this happens, turn off the burner head flame, and vigorously blow out the flame coming from the filler cap. Allow the stove to cool and *do not* open the filler cap until the stove is completely cool and the pressure in the tank is relieved.

Fuel containers. The best containers for the storage of white gasoline, kerosene, or alcohol are the cylindrical spun-aluminum bottles. Available in 1-pint and 1-quart sizes, these fuel bottles are lightweight but extremely tough. A special pouring cap is available to replace an eyedropper and funnel used in preheating and filling the tank of the camping stove. The pouring cap is simply the plastic stopper of the fuel bottle with a plastic pouring tube inserted into the stopper. When the pouring cap is placed on the fuel bottle, the flow of the fuel is controlled by covering or uncovering the vent hole with the forefinger. This control of fuel flow prevents wasted fuel and hazardous spillings. To prevent the loss of the pouring cap, tie it to the bottle stopper with a short length of nylon cord.

COOKWARE

Keep kitchen utensils as simple as possible. Cooking pots made of aluminum are the most popular, because they are lightweight and durable. Pots with lids that double as plates or pans and often nest inside one another are very space efficient. Their low profiles and broad bases also promote rapid heating. Aluminum frying pans and griddles, however, are less efficient heat spreaders than those coated with Teflon or made of steel. In any event, buy good quality aluminum cookware. Cheaper sets not only conduct heat less efficiently and occasionally warp, but they may also contain dangerous levels of lead and copper.

Dutch ovens, made of cast iron, are heavy but remain a tradition in river cooking. In the hands of an experienced cook, the Dutch oven is extremely versatile and virtually unsurpassable for cooking cobblers. Newer models of the Dutch oven, made of cast aluminum, are much lighter than the cast iron counterparts and are efficient heat conductors (without the hot spots present in ordinary aluminum when it is subjected to high temperatures). The 10-inch size is fine for smaller groups, where space and weight are crucial, or for side dishes. The 12-inch is excellent for main dishes and desserts.

In addition to the forks, spoons, and knives used for eating, other utensils are necessary. Be sure to include a can opener, serving fork, cooking spoon, serving spoon, carving knife, paring knife, turning spatula, and tongs. Another widely used and versatile piece of cookware is the stainless steel cup with a broad, flared design and wire handle (often known as a Sierra Cup). The cup can be used as a dish or cup and is designed so the rim and handle of the cup will not become uncomfortably hot in spite of its contents. The wire handle hooks securely over a belt or snaps easily onto a belt clip.

A pair of pot gripper pliers for removing pots from a fire or camping stove is also an important utensil.

DISHWASHING

All food scraps should be burned or dumped in the garbage sack and carried out. Although campfires will smudge cooking pots, this blackening can be removed easily. Simply rub the outside of these pots with soap before cooking, and when washing, rinse off the soap and the black smudge will come off with it.

When washing cookware, use two containers, one with soapy water (use biodegradable soap) for cleaning and one with clear water for sterilizing the cookware. Always boil the water in these two containers, not only to aid cleaning and sterilizing but to purify the water. To sanitize dishes, immerse them in a third container of water to which chlorine has been added. After rinsing, air the cookware if possible, or dry with clean paper towels. Dump the dishwashing water at least 100 feet from the river's high water line.

Photo courtesy of Campways

Selecting Campsites

Most river campers like to get an early morning start on the
river so they can stop earlier in the day to set up camp. With an
hour or two of daylight remaining, there is plenty of time to
unload the raft, change clothes, set up sleeping quarters, hike,
and begin supper. It is simply easier to perform these tasks in
the light of day rather than groping around in the dark with a
flashlight.

Looking for a campsite with several hours of sunlight remaining also makes it possible to be selective and find the best site
available. When dusk approaches, the rafter is practically
forced to camp wherever he can find a place to tie the raft.

Natural hazards in the area should be the first consideration
in the selection of a campsite. The campsite terrain should be
noted to check the possibility of trees and rocks falling from
loose hillsides and ledges. The campsite should allow movement
to higher ground if the river begins to rise unexpectedly. For
this reason, it is best not to camp in sheer canyons that prevent
retreat.

The possibility of a storm should be considered, and lightning recognized as a potential hazard. Hilltops, tall trees, and large, open areas are especially susceptible to lightning strikes and should be avoided when possible. It may also be important to find an area offering protection from the wind and rain. The amount of protection needed will depend on the type of tents and other shelter the camping party has. A good tent will allow comfortable camping in even the most adverse conditions, but if only a tarp or bivouac cover are available, natural shelters can become very important.

Climate plays an important part in campsite selection. In hot climates, shaded areas provide a cooler, more comfortable camp. Breezy areas are usually less infested with mosquitos and other insects. In the cooler mountain climates, flat valleys are the coldest, so set camp 100 feet or more above the valley floor if possible. It is often 10 or 15 degrees warmer than the valley itself.

If you wish to get an early start on the river, camp in an area with an opening to the east to allow the sun to hit the camp as early as possible. If you only plan to spend a couple of hours on the river the next day and wish to sleep late in the morning, camp where the mountains or canyon walls will obstruct the rising sun.

Still other factors are important in selecting your campsite. Availability of drinking water and firewood, for example, may dictate the site chosen. Or you may just wish to stop at a place where the fishing looks good.

Be sure, in addition to the other considerations, to camp in an area that offers beautiful scenery.

Sanitation

A camping party in any kind of country automatically imposes a dense population on a limited area. This concentration of use is especially emphasized in river trips that pass through a corridor of mountains or canyons, limiting the available space even further. This use has a serious impact on the river's banks and requires special consideration in sanitary measures of garbage and human waste disposal.

GARBAGE

The rule for the disposal of garbage is simple: carry it all out in a garbage bag. The best garbage bag is a heavy duty plastic bag placed inside an abrasion-resisting nylon or canvas duffle bag. Keep the garbage bag handy for use during the day. Be especially careful of cigarette butts and flip tops of aluminum cans.

If using a campfire, burn all flammable trash (aluminum foil packets will not burn). If the garbage cannot be burned, or if you are using a camping stove, dispose of garbage by placing it in the garbage bag. It is also best not to bury food scraps, for they will be dug up by animals, with the resulting scars on the banks of the river. Never bury cans or bottles; they require too much time to decompose and may be scooped up by rising river levels.

HUMAN WASTE

The proper disposal of human waste has become both a health and environmental problem in areas used for outdoor recreation. Several methods of waste disposal are possible. Smaller parties (up to four people) in remote areas may bury human waste, after burning the toilet paper, in holes six inches deep and at least 100 feet from the river's high water line. This shallow depth is best because most of the soil elements that cause rapid decomposition of organic matter lie within six inches of the surface. Waste buried deeper disintegrates very slowly. Lime or other disinfecting chemicals will counteract odor, repel flies, and most importantly, hasten decomposition. After adding these chemicals, the hole must be filled completely before leaving.

For larger groups and in heavily traveled areas, chemical toilets are a necessity to prevent environmental destruction (self-contained toilets are also required on a number of rivers administered by federal agencies). Several portable models can be used for river trips. After the water and chemicals are added to the toilet, it is ready for use. Biodegradable toilet paper should be used not only to hasten its disintegration, but also to avoid clogging the valves and pump of the toilet. The waste is then emptied and covered in a hole at least two feet deep, as well as

100 feet from the river's high water line and away from any area normally used for camping.

An alternative to the commercially available chemical toilet also exists. The wastes can be chemically sterilized and contained, placed on the raft, carried to the take-out point, and properly disposed in a landfill. The actual cost of this technique, the amount of handling of the waste, and the impact on the environment are all less than the commercial toilet. The necessary equipment for the system includes:

- 2 metal containers (such as military ammunition boxes of the 20 mm size, 19 x 8 x 14 inches)
- Plastic toilet seat with removable inside ring
- Large heavy duty plastic garbage bags
- Small heavy duty plastic garbage bags
- Formaldehyde solution (or other disinfecting chemical designed for this purpose)
- Rubber gloves

The toilet seat, garbage bags, chemicals, and rubber gloves are stored in one metal box. The other box serves as the toilet container. This box is first lined with one of the large garbage bags. Next, one of the small garbage bags is attached to the ring on the toilet seat. The toilet seat and attached bag are then placed on the box, and the chemicals are added. The toilet is now ready for use. After each use, the toilet should be covered with another large garbage bag to discourage flies and other insects.

When you are ready to leave the campsite, it only takes a few minutes to dismantle the toilet system and store the waste products. While wearing rubber gloves, the inside ring of the toilet seat should be removed and the bag containing the waste securely tied off (nylon cord works better than metal twist tabs). Because the bag containing the waste is inside the box that is lined with a large garbage bag, this large garbage bag should be tied. The lid of the box can then be sealed, and the container is ready for storage on the raft.

5

River Safety

River rafting, like many other sports, is potentially dangerous unless it is approached with foresight and a keen regard for established safety rules. Most river accidents can be prevented with the exercise of several safety precautions and river running techniques. If the occasional emergency occurs, an awareness of the appropriate methods will allow a relatively effortless rescue of persons or rafts. Likewise, a knowledge of first aid will assist in preventing and caring for accidental injuries.

Safety Precautions

The most important aspect of river safety cannot be well-defined in a list of regulations—safety consciousness. The need for establishing a serious tone concerning safety matters from the outset of the trip is very important, for a casual and cavalier attitude can easily lead to tragedy.

LEADER RESPONSIBILITIES

River Conditions. Collect detailed maps and guide books of the river. Have a reasonable knowledge of the difficulty ratings on sections of the river. Be aware of changes in the river level and how these changes affect the difficulty of the run. Obtain the approximate flow rate or river level from the proper authorities.

Participants. Inform participants of expected river conditions and determine if prospective boaters are qualified for the trip. Review safety and rescue measures.

Equipment. Plan so all necessary group equipment is included. Life jackets, rescue rope, first aid kit, spare oars and paddles, repair materials, and necessary survival equipment should be carried.

Float Plan. Plans should be filed with appropriate authorities or someone who will contact those authorities after a specified time. Determine locations of possible assistance along the river in case of emergency.

PERSONAL PREPARATION

River Knowledge. Have knowledge of your rafting ability and do not attempt rivers beyond your ability. Be aware of river hazards and avoid them. Control of the raft must be good enough to stop or reach shore before reaching danger. Do not enter a rapid unless sure you can safely negotiate it or swim the entire rapid in event of capsizing.

Life Jackets. Wear a life jacket at all times.

Clothing. Dress appropriately for the weather and water temperature. Wear tennis shoes that will protect the feet if thrown in the river or forced to walk for help.

Emergencies. Familiarize yourself with escape from an overturned raft, swimming rapids, rescue techniques, and first aid.

RAFT AND EQUIPMENT INSPECTION

Equipment Inspection. Test new and unfamiliar equipment before relying on it for difficult runs. Be sure equipment is in good repair before starting a trip.

Oars and Paddles. Use strong, adequately sized oars or paddles for controlling the raft. Carry several spares.

Life Jackets. Carry at least one extra life jacket per raft.

Raft Capacity. Respect rules for raft capacity and do not overload the raft. (See Table 3.)

Equipment Hazards. Eliminate sharp projections that could cause injury. Check to ensure that nothing will cause entanglement if the raft overturns.

Lines. Carry bow and stern lines, in addition to lines for rescue and lining. Keep lines out of the way to avoid entanglement.

Photo courtesy of Campways

Grab Lines. Provide grab lines for passengers to hold onto during the rapids and in case of upset.

Repair Materials. Carry sufficient repair materials and tie them securely to the raft.

Air Pump. Carry at least one air pump for each raft and tie it securely to the raft.

First Aid Kit and Survival Equipment. Carry sufficient first aid supplies and survival equipment according to the length and remoteness of the trip.

River Running Techniques

Most rafters travel in groups of two rafts or more in order to allow greater safety in an emergency situation. The difficult rapids are scouted from the shore, and the decision must be made whether to run the rapids or line the raft through them. If the decision is made to run the rapids, the utmost care must be taken.

A knowledge of river currents and hydraulics, as well as rowing or paddling strokes, is a necessity. To supplement these skills other river running techniques are available, including deliberate swamping and the triple rig. It may be advisable to station rescue rope throwers along the run. For safety reasons, it may be best to have some of the passengers walk around the rapids. To further lighten the load of the raft and increase its maneuverability, equipment and gear may be carried around the rapids.

If the rapids are extremely difficult and if the run would jeopardize the safety of the passengers, the raft should be lined around the rapids.

TABLE 3
Raft Capacity for Persons and Gear

Raft Size	Rafts With Frames and Oars		Paddle Rafts	
	With Gear	Without Gear	With Gear	Without Gear
6-Man (12'x6')	2	3	3	4
7-Man (13'x6'8")	3	4-5	4	4-5
10-Man (15'x7'6")	4	5-6	6	6
14-Man (17'x8')	5-6	6-7	8	8

GROUP TRAVEL

The raft with the most experienced rower or paddling crew leads the way while another competent crew brings up the rear as the sweep raft. Each raft should keep the one behind it in sight at all times.

Although generally close together, the rafts should greatly increase the distance between each other while running rapids. Crowding together in rapids not only restricts maneuverability but also provides the possibility of one raft colliding into another and forcing it against a river obstacle (commonly known as a "raft sandwich"). A raft following another should allow sufficient distance that, if the preceding raft encounters trouble, it can stop before entering the rapids.

Group travel allows for the rescue of passengers and rafts if an emergency develops. Each rafter, after running the rapids, can establish a position for the potential rescue of the following raft.

DELIBERATE SWAMPING

In large rapids where the overturning of a raft is a real possibility, many rafters fill the raft with water, rendering it so heavy that it is practically impossible for the rapids to flip it. The raft can be filled with buckets or by taking small waves sideways. This technique of deliberate swamping, however, should be used only in deep water containing large waves and reversals without rocks. This is because a raft full of water is not only sluggish to maneuver but is vulnerable to damage by those rocks.

TRIPLE RIG

Three rafts may be lashed together to provide additional stability in extremely large rapids that are easily capable of overturning a single raft. Although not as maneuverable as an individual raft, the triple rig—with each raft running sideways downstream—is best controlled with sweep oars extending from the sides of the bow and stern rafts.

The primary danger associated with these rafts is the possibility of the downstream raft flipping back onto the center raft (known as "pancaking"). To prevent this dangerous situation, a line should be attached underneath the rafts, beginning from the downstream side of the bow raft and extending to the stern side of the middle raft. A little extra weight in the downstream raft will also deter this hazard.

LINING AND PORTAGING

If the decision is made not to run the rapids, it is then necessary to line the raft through, or portage around, the rapids. Lining a raft requires controlling it from the shore with bow and stern lines. Before lining, always lash down all gear securely. In rocky stretches of the river, lining becomes difficult because of the tight maneuvering between rocks. In shallow areas it is often essential to have someone push the raft along or further into the current, while others maintain control with the lines attached to the raft. In sections of the river with powerful currents and no obstructions, the raft may be allowed to float, with lines still attached but slackened, to the calm water below the rapids.

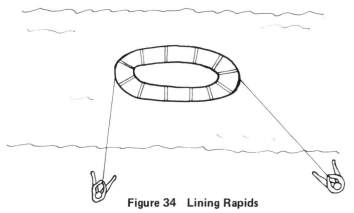

Figure 34   Lining Rapids

Rescue and Emergencies

Emergencies can occur at anytime. While each situation is unique, a few basic principles are easily applied to accomplish self-rescue, rescue of others, or rescue of rafts. To be prepared for extreme emergencies requiring outside assistance, signaling equipment is necessary. A survival kit should be included for trips in extremely remote areas.

SWIMMING RAPIDS

When swimming rapids, the swimmer should face downstream with feet extended in order to ward off oncoming rocks. In heavy waves, take a breath whenever possible and hold it while submerged.

If a large reversal or rock lies downstream, the swimmer should begin swimming across the river early enough to evade the obstacle. One should be especially careful to avoid reversals which are capable of trapping and rolling the swimmer. But if you find you are headed toward a reversal, take a deep breath and relax. In most instances, the reversal will pull you underwater and into the underlying current which is moving downstream. The life jacket will bring you back to the surface.

The swimmer should be especially careful to avoid being pinned between a rock and the raft. Always stay away from the raft's downstream side. After swimming to the foot of the rapids, you should move toward the shore or into an eddy, allowing the raft to pick you up after it has run the rapids.

RESCUE OF RAFTERS

In most instances, a person who falls out of the raft is able to swim through the rapids and walk to shore or climb aboard the raft. In strong currents, however, it is often advisable to have safety lines ready downstream for the rescue of those who are unable to swim ashore.

A number of lines made especially for rescue purposes are now commercially available. Most are about sixty feet in length and are made of 3/8-inch braided polyethylene (because it floats). A brightly colored line is best because it is more visible in the water. Some lines contain floats to aid in throwing, but these floats may become entangled in the rocks of the river.

Prior to its use, the rescue line should be coiled; one half of the coil is held in one hand and one half in the other hand. The first coil should be thrown while the second coil is allowed to feed out freely (with the remaining end held securely in the hand). For the best accuracy, throw the coil with an underhand motion.

The placement of the line in the water is very important. The line should be thrown slightly downstream from the swimmer's position because the swimmer is moving with the current. After the swimmer grabs the rescue line, a tremendous pull will be exerted on the line. The rescuer should belay the line around the waist or a nearby tree, sitting down for additional bracing. If the swimmer, failing to catch the line, continues downstream, it may be necessary to follow with a raft.

RESCUE OF RAFTS

In shallow rivers the raft may become lodged on a rock or gravel bar, but it is normally easy to push the raft off of the obstacle. The raft may collide with large boulders that protrude above the river's surface. If the raft is headed toward one of these boulders, it is best to strike it with the bow of the raft; in this way, the current of the river, with the aid of a few rowing or paddling strokes, will usually swing the raft off the rock.

If a sideways collision with the rock (known as broaching) is unavoidable, a few precautions should be taken in order to prevent swamping the raft. The rushing current has the tendency to pull the upstream tube down and eventually submerge it, so people in the raft should jump to the downstream side of the raft, lifting the upstream tube slightly out of the water.

To move the broached raft from the rock, several methods should be attempted until one of them succeeds. First, have the occupants shift their weight to the side of the raft that is most likely to spin off the rock. Or, it may be possible to manually push the raft away from the rock. Try swinging an oar into the main current to act as a lever that will catch the force of the current. If these methods fail, attach lines to the raft and pull from the shore.

If the raft's upstream tube is pulled underwater and the raft becomes "wrapped" around a rock, rescue becomes more difficult. If the raft is wrapped on a large rock, it may be possible to stand on the rock and pull the raft up and out of the water. If this procedure is not possible or does not succeed, attach lines to several points on the raft's bow and stern and pull these lines from the shore. If these methods fail, deflate the section that is under the greatest pressure and pull on the inflated section. The deflation should reduce much of the weight and pressure of the water which is held inside the raft by the inflated tubes.

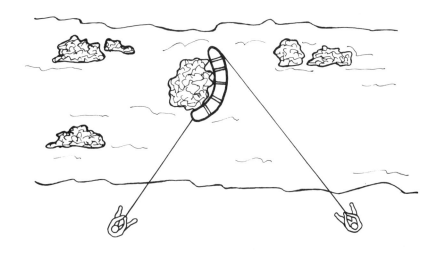

Figure 35   Rescue of a Wrapped Raft

EMERGENCY EQUIPMENT

In addition to a rescue line, signaling and survival equipment may be required for extreme emergencies. Be sure to attach this equipment securely so it will not be lost if the raft overturns.

Signaling devices. In some instances signals may be necessary in order to obtain outside assistance. A small signaling mirror with center sighting hole is the least expensive method. Other signaling devices are available to attract attention. These devices include flares, brightly colored or reflective panels, flashing lights with strong beams, and red "smoke."

Survival kit. In more remote areas it is advisable to carry a survival kit. A compass and topographic map of the surrounding area should always be included in case it is necessary to walk for help. Waterproof matches, a knife, fish hooks and line are useful. Emergency or "space" blankets, made of a sheet of laminated polyethylene, aluminum, and fiberglass, can be used as a wind- and rain-proof shelter. They can also serve to prevent body heat loss.

6

First Aid

Accidental injuries and sudden illness may be aggravated by the remoteness of the river party from professional medical services. It is important that several members of the trip are trained in first aid techniques, and an advanced first aid book should be included with the first aid kit. The following discussion of first aid is intended only as a refresher course for the more common conditions that require the administration of fast and efficient first aid procedures. For more remote trips, a physician should be consulted for suggestions concerning the medical care of more serious injuries or illness.

HYPOTHERMIA

Hypothermia, very simply, is the loss of body heat that results in a lowering in the temperature of the body's vital core. This loss of body heat can result in uncontrollable shivering, followed by increasing clumsiness, loss of judgment, and finally, unconsciousness and death.

Heat loss caused by the conduction of heat away from the body by wet clothing is the most serious cause of concern for the rafter. Because water has 240 times the thermal conductivity of still air, total immersion in the river results in extremely rapid progression of symptoms, allowing very little time for treatment. Even after rescue, heat loss will continue as a result of evaporation, especially if it is windy. An external source of heat (such as another persons's body heat or a campfire) is necessary to revive the victim. Blankets and coverings do not help to replace body heat, but only reduce the loss of heat which has already occurred.

Precautions.

• Because muscular activity produces body heat that allows the body to replace lost heat, maintaining a high level of activity will permit an individual to withstand more cold.

• Provide a high calorie intake so energy is available to maintain muscular activity.

• Avoid becoming exhausted. In such a weakened condition one is especially susceptible to hypothermia.

• Dress for the weather with proper wind and water protection.

• Never allow hypothermia the chance to progress. The first symptoms should be treated seriously, not just as someone being cold. Progression from shivering to heart failure may occur in less than two hours.

Symptoms.

• Shivering becomes intense and uncontrollable. Ability to perform complex tasks is impaired.

• Violent shivering persists. Difficulty in speaking, sluggish thinking, and amnesia begin to appear.

• Shivering decreases and is replaced by strong muscular rigidity. Muscle coordination is affected, producing erratic or jerky movements. Thinking is less clear. General comprehension of the situation is dulled and may be accompanied by total amnesia. The victim is generally still able to maintain posture and the appearance of psychological contact with his surroundings.

• Victim becomes irrational, loses contact with the environment, and drifts into stupor. Muscular rigidity continues. Pulse and respiration are slowed.

• Unconsciousness follows. Victim does not respond to speech. Most reflexes cease to function at this temperature level. Heartbeat becomes erratic.

• Failure of cardiac and respiratory control centers in the brain. Cardiac fibrillation. Probable edema and hemorrhage in lungs, then death.

Treatment.

- Get the victim out of the water and into whatever shelter may be available.
- Replace wet or damp clothing.
- Insulate the victim from the ground.
- Warm the victim by the best method available. The victim is usually incapable of producing sufficient body heat to warm himself. Heat from a supplemental source must be provided. If it is not possible to build a fire, body heat from other members of the party should be used. For the maximum transfer of heat, the people should be as lightly clad as possible.
- An unconscious victim should be placed in a supine position with the head tilted back to maintain an open air passage for breathing.
- A conscious victim should be given warm fluids. If the victim can eat, feed food high in carbohydrates.
- No alcohol should be given to the victim. It may cause a sudden release of cold blood from the body's surface to the body's core.

ARTIFICIAL RESPIRATION

When breathing stops from any cause, begin artificial respiration at once.

- Place victim on back. Turn victim's head to the side and wipe any visible foreign matter from the mouth.
- Tilt the victim's head backward so the chin is pointing upward. Push jaw into jutting out position to prevent tongue from blocking air passage.
- Pinch victim's nostrils shut.
- Blow air into the victim's mouth.
- Watch victim's chest to see when it rises. Stop blowing when the chest is expanded. Remove your mouth and listen for exhalation.
- Repeat breathing, removing your mouth each time to allow the escape of air. Provide at least one breath every five seconds.

- If you are not getting an air exchange, recheck the position of the head and jaw, and check to see if foreign matter in the back of the mouth may be obstructing the air passage. If foreign matter is preventing ventilation, as a last resort, turn the victim on his side and administer sharp blows between the shoulder blades to dislodge the material.

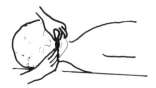

Place victim on back. If there is anything in the victim's mouth, turn head to side and quickly wipe it out with your fingers.

Straighten victim's head and tilt back so chin points up. Push jaw up to jutting out position to keep tongue from blocking air passage.

Place your mouth tightly over victim's and pinch nostrils shut. Breath into victim's mouth until chest rises. Remove your mouth. Listen for the sound of returning air.

BLEEDING

To stop severe bleeding. Apply direct pressure by placing the palm of the hand with a dressing over the entire area of the wound. If blood soaks through the dressing, do not remove it, but rather add additional layers of dressing and continue direct pressure. Unless there is evidence of a fracture, a seriously bleeding open wound of the neck, hand, arms, or leg should be elevated.

If severe bleeding from an open wound of the arm or leg does not stop after the application of direct pressure and elevation, the pressure point technique may be required. Do not substitute the use of a pressure point for direct pressure and elevation but use the pressure point in addition to those techniques. Do not use a pressure point any longer than necessary to stop the bleeding.

If the previous methods do not control severe bleeding and if the victim is in danger of bleeding to death, the tourniquet may be used *as a last resort* to save life. This method is used only on the arm or leg, and once a tourniquet is applied, care by a physician is imperative. To apply, place the tourniquet just above the wound but not touching the wound edges. If the wound is in a joint area or just below, place the tourniquet slightly above the joint. Wrap the tourniquet band tightly twice around the limb and tie a half knot. Place a short stick on the half knot, then tie a full knot. Twist the stick until the bleeding has stopped and secure the stick in place with a bandage. Attach a note to the victim that relates the location of the tourniquet and the time it was applied. Treat for shock and seek medical attention immediately. *Once the serious decision to apply a tourniquet has been made, the tourniquet should not be loosened except on the advice of a physician.*

Chest wounds. When anything penetrates the chest deeply, air may be heard passing in and out of the wound, often causing a sucking sound. Unless this air exchange is stopped, the lung may collapse. To prevent this air exchange and the loss of blood place a thick pad of sterile gauze or clean cloth over the wound. Bind the pad tightly in place with adhesive tape or a bandage (preferably elastic) around the chest. The binding should be snug enough to hold the dressing firmly in place, but not so tight that it will unduly restrict breathing.

Abdominal wounds. Control bleeding with a pressure dressing—preferably a sterile gauze pad—held firmly in place. If intestines protrude from the wound, the dressing must be kept moist with lukewarm water. Keep the victim warm and lying on back with the knees bent.

BONE AND JOINT INJURIES

When giving first aid for broken bones or fractures, do no more than safeguard the victim against further injury. Keep the victim comfortable and take steps to prevent shock. Never attempt to set a broken bone. In general, there are two kinds of fractures, closed and open. In a closed fracture the bone is broken but it does not pierce the skin to cause an external wound. In an open fracture the bone is broken and causes a wound as the bone protrudes through the skin.

Closed fracture. Place the limb in as natural a position as possible without causing discomfort to the victim. Do not move the victim until splints have been applied. Splints must be long enough to extend well beyond the joint and below the fracture. Use any firm material as a splint, and pad the splint with clothing or other soft material to prevent skin injury. Fasten splints with a bandage or cloth.

Open fracture. Do not clean the wound. Apply pressure with a dressing to control bleeding. Hold the pad in place with a bandage. Keep the victim lying down. Apply a splint, but do not attempt to set a fracture or push a protruding bone end back. Elevate the limb slightly to reduce hemorrhage and swelling.

Dislocations. A dislocation is a displacement of a bone end from the joint (particularly at the shoulder, elbow, or fingers). Never attempt to reduce a dislocation or correct any deformity near a joint. Splint and immobilize the affected joint in the position in which it is found.

Sprains and strains. A sprain results when ligaments supporting a joint or connecting bones are overstretched or torn. The sprain is usually accompanied by pain, swelling, and discoloration, but it is generally impossible to differentiate a sprain from a closed fracture without an x-ray. A strain, likewise, is similar to a sprain but it involves muscles rather than ligaments. Treat both sprains and strains the same. Place the injured part at rest, elevate it if possible, and apply cold compresses or ice packs for several hours. Do not apply heat in any form to a sprain or strain unless a doctor advises.

BURNS

Burns are usually classified according to the depth or degree of skin damage. Often the degree will differ in various parts of the same affected area. First degree burns are usually red or discolored with mild swelling and pain. Second degree burns are characterized by red or mottled appearance, development of blisters, considerable swelling, and a wet appearance of the surface of the skin. This is due to the loss of plasma through the damaged layers of the skin. The usual signs of third degree burns are deep tissue destruction, white or charred appearance, and complete loss of all layers of the skin.

First degree burns. Use cold water application or submerge burned area in cold water. Apply dry sterile dressing. Do not apply butter or margarine to burn.

Second degree burns. Immerse in cold water. Apply dry sterile dressing. Treat for shock. Do not break blisters or remove shreds of tissue. Do not use antiseptic ointment or spray.

Third degree burns. Apply dry sterile dressing. Treat for shock. If the hands are burned, keep them above the level of the heart. Keep burned legs or feet elevated. Watch for breathing difficulty. If medical help is not available within an hour, give the victim a weak solution of salt and soda (one teaspoon of salt and one-half teaspoon of baking soda to each quart of water). Do not remove charred clothing that is stuck to the burn. Do not apply ice or other antiseptic preparations.

SHOCK

Shock is a condition where vital bodily functions are depressed because of an insufficient flow of blood through the body. Since shock may accompany any severe injury or emotional disturbance, it is best to expect some degree of shock, either mild or severe, with any accident or medical emergency. If a state of shock continues over several hours, it may be fatal or cause permanent damage to the brain or other organs.

Several symptoms will result. The skin is pale (or bluish), moist, and clammy. The pulse is usually quite rapid and while often too faint to be felt at the wrist, it is perceptible in the carotid artery at the side of the neck. The rate of breathing is usually increased, and it can be shallow, possibly deep, and irregular. A victim in shock from hemorrhage may become restless and anxious, thrash about, and complain of severe thirst. The victim may also vomit and feel nauseous.

A victim whose condition is deteriorating may reveal other symptoms. The victim may become apathetic and unresponsive and his eyes may be sunken, with a vacant expression, and the pupils widely dilated. Some of the blood vessels in the skin may be dilated, producing a mottled appearance which indicates the victim's blood pressure has fallen to a very low level. If untreated, the victim usually loses consciousness, the body temperature falls, and the victim may die.

The steps for preventing shock and administering first aid include:

- Keep the victim lying down.
- Cover the victim *only* enough to prevent loss of body heat.
- A victim with a head injury should not have the head lower than the rest of the body. Otherwise, the victim may improve if the feet are raised from eight to twelve inches.
- Fluids may be given if medical care is delayed an hour or more. Give the victim a weak solution of salt and soda (one teaspoon of salt and one-half teaspoon of baking soda to each quart of water).

SNAKEBITES

- Immobilize the arm or leg in a lowered position, keeping the area involved below the level of the victim's heart.
- Apply a constricting band from two to four inches above the bite, between the bite and the victim's heart. The constricting band should not be too tight; if it is properly adjusted, there will be some oozing from the wound.
- Use the blade in the snakebite kit to cut short incision marks through the skin at the fang mark and slightly below those marks.
- Apply suction with the suction cup contained in the snakebite kit.
- Wash the wound thoroughly with soap and water, and apply a dry sterile dressing. A cold, wet cloth may be applied to the bite to slow the body's absorption of the venom.

HEAT STROKE AND EXHAUSTION

Heat stroke and heat exhaustion are entirely different conditions, even though both result from the same cause—exposure to extreme heat. The symptoms of heat stroke include very hot and dry skin. Symptoms of heat exhaustion include cold and clammy skin.

Heat stroke. Move victim to shade and undress to underwear. Cool the victim's body by sponging with cool water or rubbing alcohol. Take care, however, to avoid over-chilling the victim once body temperature has been sufficiently reduced.

Heat exhaustion. Have victim lie down, with feet raised from eight to twelve inches. Loosen tight clothing, and after moving the victim to shade, apply cool, wet cloths. Give the victim sips of salt water (one teaspoon of salt per glass, every fifteen minutes), over a period of about one hour.

FIRST AID KIT

Adhesive compress (1, 2 and, 4 inch)
Gauze pads (3 and 4 inch squares)
Gauze roller bandage (3 inches x 5 yards)
Triangular bandages
Burn ointment/spray
Antiseptic
Aspirin
Eye dressing kit
Tourniquet
Scissors
Tweezers
Cotton swabs
Snake bite kit
Adhesive tape
Band-Aids
Splints
Ammonia inhalents
Sunburn lotion
Ace bandage (2 x 5 yards)
Butterfly closures
Razor blades
Safety pins
Moleskin
Salt tablets
Oil of cloves (toothache)
Visine/Murine
Antiseptic towlettes
Calamine lotion
Antihistamine (hay fever, stings)
Syrup of Ipecac
Antacid

7

Equipment Maintenance and Repair

River running is tough on rafts and its related rafting and camping equipment, but most well-made equipment, with regular maintenance, will endure punishment for many seasons. Proper care of rafting gear will not only prolong its useful life but will help ensure its safety for use on the river.

Raft Maintenance

With reasonable care, a river raft will last for many years, and some of the better models will endure almost indefinitely. Several precautions, however, will lengthen the life of the raft and reduce the number of repairs needed.

The most common cause of ordinary wear on a raft results from the abrasion of the frame as it rubs against the top of the raft's buoyancy tubes. This wear may be reduced considerably by padding the frame in areas where it comes in contact with the raft, or by gluing additional layers of coated fabric onto the raft in contact areas.

One should never step on or drag an uninflated raft on the ground because of the possibility of puncturing it. Care should be taken while inflating the raft. Only enough air should first be added to each air chamber to hold the raft "softly" in shape. The raft can then be topped off to its proper operating pressure. Because a raft's chambers are separated by bulkheads, or bladders, this procedure relieves the stress that can occur when one chamber is over-inflated. Over-inflation of one chamber can cause the bladder to balloon into the next chamber. With-out any counterbalancing support from the air of the adjacent chamber, the bladder may tear.

When inflating a raft, add air until the buoyancy tube is drum tight—or at the point when the fist bounces off the tube when striking it. This places air pressure at about 2 pounds per square inch (p.s.i.), which is the correct operating pressure for most rafts. An air pressure gauge can be used, and it provides a more precise measurement. Because the bursting pressure of most well-made rafts is between 8 and 12 p.s.i., the pressure of the raft may increase somewhat without any danger. In a hot climate, however, if a raft is inflated in the cool of the morning and is left in the hot sun, the air expands and it becomes neces-sary to release air in order to prevent unnecessary strain on the seams and valves of the raft.

Before deflating a raft at the end of a trip, stand it on one side at the river's edge and wash it out by splashing buckets of water into it, taking special care to wash away small rocks lodged between the buoyancy tubes and the floor. If the rocks are not removed, they may puncture the raft while it is rolled up for storage. Only mild soap and water should be used to remove dirt. Harsh detergents, as well as petroleum products, tend to disintegrate the raft's coating. Commercial rubber preservatives containing silicone should not be used. This is because silicone causes the surface of the raft to become slippery, making it im-possible to apply adhesives in case of repair.

Upon returning home, the raft should be aired out and com-pletely dry before storing. If not, the excess water will weaken the seams of the raft, especially those surrounding the floor. As a result, the floor may fall completely out of the raft. It is also important to remove any water that may have found its way into the inside of a buoyancy tube (which usually occurs when there is a tear in the fabric). Valves should not be closed but open—to allow air to circulate in the tubes. Rot and mildew, caused by even the slightest amount of moisture, can be pre-vented by sprinkling talcum powder over the raft. The raft should then be rolled up loosely with a small amount of air re-maining in the buoyancy tubes. Never fold the raft tightly for an extended period of time because the tension creates undue stress on the fabric of the coated material. Lastly, the raft should be wrapped in a tarp and stored in a cool, dry place, free of rodents.

Reconditioning of Rafts

Despite this careful maintenance, a raft may require reconditioning after several seasons of scraping against rocks. Mildly worn areas of the raft that are not exposed to possible chafing by rocks can be painted with an appropriate coating to prevent additional wear. Heavily abraded areas, and lightly abraded areas on the raft's bottom and sides, should be patched with additional material. The parts of the raft that contact the frame also chafe, and should be painted or patched for additional protection.

Although coating compounds never offer the same resistance to abrasion as the original coating (they are not cured in a static and heat-controlled environment), they do offer protection for areas of the coating that are slightly abraded without the exposure of the fabric's threads. Be sure the coating is appropriate to the fabric to which it is applied and that the fabric contains that same type of coating (neoprene, Hypalon, PVC, or urethane).

To apply these coatings, first inflate the raft just enough to hold it "softly" in shape, then wipe the raft with a light coating of solvent. The solvent will establish a "tack" on the surface. The coating should be applied immediately to take advantage of this tack, which provides a tight bond between the coating and the raft's surface. Successive applications of the coating should be made about an hour apart for best results. Do not wait more than two or three hours, or the final coat will wrinkle.

The best method of applying these coatings is a paint roller. A paint brush may be used to touch up areas not accessible to the roller. While this coating can be used without thinner, a mixture containing twenty-five to thirty percent thinner is commonly used. It is important that the coating dry rapidly, lest the solvent it contains loosen the seams and patches of the raft. If possible, apply the coating in the direct sun, preferably in an area with a breeze.

After applying the coating, leave the raft inflated for at least a week if possible. If it must be deflated sooner, completely sprinkle the raft with talcum powder to prevent the coated surfaces from sticking together. This can occur even after the coating is dry in appearance.

Repairing Rafts

The repair of inflatable rafts involves the utilization of a few basic principles that are essential to ensure properly functioning equipment. Repairs usually involve nothing more than a simple patch, but it may be necessary to sew the tear if it is several inches in length. A repair may be adequate for the duration of the trip, but later repairs may be required for a more complete job.

Subject to minor alterations for the individual trip, the basic raft repair kit should include the following items:

- Patching material
- Solvent
- Rasp or sandpaper (for neoprene- and Hypalon-coated rafts)
- Roller
- Scissors
- Needle and thread
- Hole puncher
- Troweling compound (or silicone rubber sealant)

PATCHING

Small tears in the fabric of the raft—usually not larger than an inch or two—may be repaired by a simple patch placed on the outside of the tear. For longer tears it is advisable to first fasten a patch inside the raft before applying the outside patch to obtain the most secure patch possible. When the raft is needed for immediate service and there is not enough time to apply an inside patch, the material should be sewn in order to strengthen the area before a patch is applied. If desired, the stitching may be removed after the trip is completed and a double patch applied.

Finding the Leak. It is often difficult to determine the exact location of the leak. The best method of detecting small tears and pinpoint holes is to wipe soapy water over the surface of the raft. Any leaks in the raft's buoyancy tubes will cause air bubbles. This use of soapy water is also beneficial after the patch is applied to ensure the repair is airtight.

After the tear is located, the patch should be cut out of a sheet of the coated fabric, and preferably, the patching material should be similar in weight and coating to the material of the raft. On most extended trips, approximately one square yard of patching material should be included in case extensive repairs are required. On smaller tears (two inches or less) the patch should overlap the tear at least one inch in each direction. Larger tears will require more overlap to prevent the patch from blistering. The edges of the patch should be rounded off, since square edges are easily pulled off by objects which the patch later contacts.

Neoprene or Hypalon. In the case of neoprene- or Hypalon-coated rafts, the preparation of the surfaces to be patched is extremely important. The area around the tear, as well as the patch itself, should be scuffed or abraded to provide an interlock between the coated fabric and the adhesive. These surfaces may be buffed with a rasp, sandpaper, or a piece of steel wool saturated with paint thinner. If neither is available, natural sources, such as a piece of sandstone or other abrasive rock, are suitable. *Caution:* Do not buff deep enough to expose the underlying fabric. If the raft has been painted with a neoprene or Hypalon coating, it is essential to remove the layer of coating completely from the area to be patched. PVC and urethane are a different order of chemical, and should never be buffed prior to patching.

It is then necessary to clean the surfaces to be patched with a suitable solvent. This solvent softens the coating of the material and permits a stronger bond with the adhesive. Solvents should be water-free and be used sparingly. If they are used in excessive quantities the solvent can actually destroy the existing coating. Solvents containing naphtha or toluene can be used on neoprene/Hypalon coatings, while a solvent known simply as "MEK" or solvents containing acetone work best with PVC/urethane coatings. Regardless of the solvent used, it should be used with care because of its strong fumes and high flammability.

Adhesives. Opinions differ as to which adhesive is the best, but several good brands are available. They include Gaco, Carboline, and Bostic. These adhesives are basically similar, but vary according to the time necessary for the adhesive to cure before applying the patch. Although almost any adhesive and fabric coating will fasten together, one brand of adhesive may adhere more securely to a particular fabric coating than another brand. Gaco, for example, bonds better to neoprene-coated materials (as used in rafts manufactured by Rubber Crafters of West Virginia and Mountain State Inflatables) than other brands. Carboline adheres best with a neoprene/Hypalon combination (as used in Campways, Rogue Inflatables and Zodiac rafts), and Bostic is best suited for surfaces with a high percentage of Hypalon (as used in Avon rafts). Special urethane adhesives, on the other hand, are more compatible with materials coated with PVC and urethane (as used in Maravia rafts).

If possible, it is best to avoid extremes in air temperature when applying the adhesive. An optimum temperature is about 75 degrees for most adhesives, but conditions for patching may be modified, to some extent, to account for deviations in the temperature. For example, in warmer temperatures it may be necessary to apply more adhesive (since it dries faster) or to provide shade over the area to be glued. More difficult problems occur when the temperature is cold, for the adhesive may remain sticky and never completely dry.

Adhesive should then be applied to the area surrounding the tear and to the patch itself. The adhesive should be applied evenly. Although a thin layer is usually sufficient, only experience with a particular brand will reveal the necessary thickness. After the first layer of adhesive has dried completely, a second layer should be applied.

The time to secure the patch to the raft varies according to the brand of adhesive. The instructions on most containers of adhesive advise when the surfaces should be pressed together. In the case of Gaco adhesive, best results are achieved when allowing the adhesive to cure one-to-one and a half hours before applying the patch. Carboline adhesive should dry thirty minutes to one hour before application. The curing period for Bostic adhesive varies according to the amount of accelerator added to the adhesive.

In any case the adhesive should be slightly beyond the tacky stage before applying the patch. To determine this moment, place your finger on the patch. The patch should not stick to the finger. If it does, the adhesive should be allowed to cure longer before pressing the two surfaces together.

Before fastening the patch to the raft, it may be necessary to deflate the entire section of the raft where the repair is to be made. This will permit easier access to the area, as well as allowing the patch to be pressed down securely. After the patch has been placed on the surface of the raft, the patch must be pressed down with a roller or other hard object. Start rolling or pressing from the middle of the patch and move toward the edges. This technique will remove any air bubbles trapped under the patch. Careful attention should be given to pressing down the edges of the patch. After pressing down the patch, spread adhesive around the edges of the patch to secure it even further.

If possible, allow the adhesive to cure overnight before reinflating the damaged chamber. If not, the patch will suffice for the remainder of the trip, but later the tear should be re-patched for a stronger repair. To remove an old patch for later repairs, direct the heat of a 1,000-watt (or more) hair dryer over the area and pull the patch off with a pair of pliers.

SUMMARY OF RAFT REPAIR

- Cut patch to fit. Patch should extend at least one inch beyond the damaged area in all directions. Round corners of the patch.
- In the case of neoprene/Hypalon coatings, buff patch and the area to be patched with a rasp or coarse sandpaper. *Caution:* Do not buff deep enough to expose the threads of the fabric.
- Clean areas with a suitable solvent.
- Apply two coats of adhesive to both areas, allowing the first coat to dry completely before applying the second coat. Allow second coat to dry until the surfaces are slightly beyond the "tacky" stage.
- Apply patch to the area, being careful not to trap air under the patch.
- Roll the patch down with a roller or other hard object.

SEWING

For more extensive repairs the material should be sewn before patching. First use a hole puncher to form small parallel holes on both sides of the tear. A large curved needle, as used in upholstery repair or bookbinding, can be used for sewing the tear, and any heavy nylon thread, such as waxed dental floss, works well. The tear should be sewn with a baseball stitch,

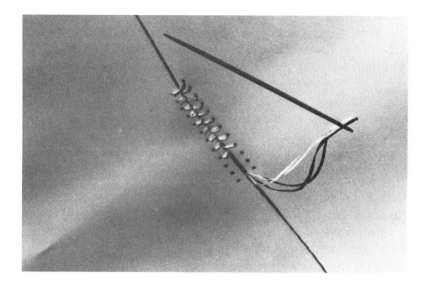

which is simply an over-and-under stitch. After the sewing is completed, the thread should not be tied off, but rather slipped through the last five or six rows of stitching before the thread is cut.

Once the tear is sewn, a patch may be applied directly over the stitching, making sure the adhesive saturates between the stitches for a better bond. (Many rafters do not recommend sewing the tear, claiming the repair is weakened by the stitching's irregularity on the surface of the patch.) Many rafters apply a sealing compound over the stitching to ensure air tightness. Troweling compound (a type of neoprene putty) may be used on neoprene surfaces, while silicone rubber sealant is useful for other coated fabrics.

If the tear is more than a foot or so in length, a process known as cold bonding may be utilized on neoprene-coated rafts instead of sewing the tear. Cold bonding must be made after the trip is completed, as it involves applying cold bond (a neoprene adhesive) to the damaged area, then several layers of cheesecloth, and finally another layer of cold bond. This cold bonding process, properly completed, is practically a reconstruction of the raft's material.

REPAIRS WITH NEOPRENE/HYPALON COATINGS

Pinpoint holes and small tears in a raft's neoprene- or Hypalon-coated material can be easily repaired with neoprene or Hypalon coatings. For pinpoint holes, deflate the raft and wipe the area of seepage with an appropriate solvent. Apply three or four coats of the coating in patches of about two square inches over each seep hole. These coats should be applied in a short period of time in order to improve adhesion. The first coat should be well brushed into the surface of the raft.

Small tears in the material of the raft can be repaired by placing a light fabric, such as cheesecloth, on the wet coating. Several layers of cloth, each slightly larger than the preceding one, will increase the strength of the repair, and sufficient coats should be applied to fill the cloth weave. If possible, allow the coating to dry a week before rolling the raft for storage. If the raft must be rolled up sooner, dust the repaired area with talcum powder to prevent the fresh coating from sticking to the raft.

Other Equipment

Rafters seem to become attached to equipment that has given them seasons of hard and reliable service. Because of this attachment (and perhaps a desire to save money), most rafters constantly maintain and repair their equipment to avoid, as long as possible, the eventual scrapping of that equipment.

FRAMES

In case of repair, wooden frames are easier to replace and repair with natural sources than metal frames. A broken board of the wooden frame may be set in a "splint" with a piece of driftwood or a tree limb as the reinforcement. This splinted area can be wound with duct tape or nylon cord to hold the support in place.

A metal frame, on the other hand, is more difficult to repair if the welding breaks. Several feet of soft metal baling wire and a roll of duct tape should be included in the repair kit for this possibility. These frame repairs are usually sufficient to enable the frame to function for the remainder of the trip.

OARS AND PADDLES

Unfinished wooden oars and paddles should first receive a coat of linseed oil to help prevent cracking, and then several coats of marine spar varnish or marine paint should be applied. After sanding the area lightly, the blades should be wrapped with fiberglass tape. Use three- or four-inch fiberglass tape saturated with fiberglass resin and wind around the blade with an overlapping motion. *Note:* Use only epoxy resins for hardwoods and not polyester resins—they disintegrate the wood.

Even good quality oars are easily broken, so it is advisable to carry two spares. Repair in the field is difficult, due to the time necessary for epoxy glue and fiberglass resin to cure. Upon returning home, more complete repairs can then be made.

Splits and breaks in wooden shafts should first be rejoined with epoxy glue, and duct tape can be used to secure the two pieces in place while the glue dries. For added strength, fiberglass tape saturated with epoxy resin should be wound around the damaged area. Apply the tape six inches above and below the break.

A hollow aluminum shaft can be repaired by sawing off the jagged edges of the shaft near the break and then inserting a tight-fitting hardwood plug into the shaft (about four inches long for paddles and ten inches for oars). This plug should be glued into the shaft and the shaft wrapped with fiberglass tape. Although the resulting oar or paddle will be a couple of inches shorter, it will work fine.

The tips of wooden oars and paddles can develop splits. These splits can be repaired by cutting out a rectangle around the split and then gluing a new hardwood rectangle into the resulting gap. Fiberglass tape will give the area additional reinforcement.

VALVES

Ordinary dirt is the greatest enemy of raft valves as it finds its way into the interior of the valve, causing abrasion of the valve parts and stickiness of movement. To reduce this wear, periodically clean out the valve with a toothbrush and soapy water.

If the valve or its gasket leaks, it is preferable to replace the valve, since valve repairs are usually not long-lasting. Peter and Russel one-piece valves, as well as I.T.T., Campways, and other similar valves, are simple to replace—simply unscrew the screws surrounding the valve.

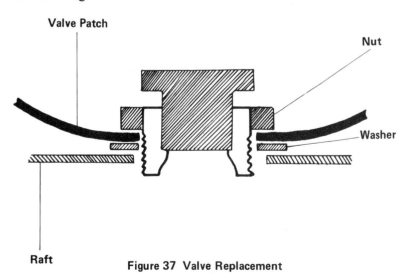

Figure 37 Valve Replacement

The Bridgeport-Schraeder and other two-piece valves are more difficult to repair, for the entire valve patch must be replaced. To replace these valves, first cut the old valve out of the raft. After buffing and applying adhesive to the surfaces to be covered, place a new valve and its surrounding patch onto the raft.

The area surrounding the valve may also leak, usually the result of an object hitting the valve and causing a tear in the raft's material. If the tear occurs at the edge of the valve, troweling compound or silicone rubber can be applied to seal the leak. Other tears in the fabric may be glued and patched with material in the conventional manner.

"D" RINGS

Occasionally the tremendous stress on a "D" ring will cause the ring to tear apart from the patch. To repair these, cut new strips of nylon webbing or coated fabric, and glue these strips, with the ring inserted, to the rear patch. Then cut a rectangular slit in the larger front patch to enable the "D" ring to pass through this front patch. Place glue on the sides of the patches to be fastened, and then press securely together.

These same procedures can be followed to manufacture "D" ring patches from scratch. This will save a considerable amount of money when compared with the price of the finished product.

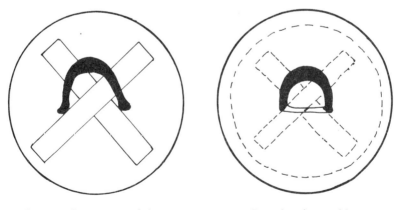

Rear patch, straps, and rings   Completed assembly

Figure 38 "D" Ring Repair

AIR PUMPS

To prevent rust and provide ease of operation, all air pumps should be lubricated regularly. Most well-made cylinder pumps are durable products, and their simple design enables easy repair. The repairs needed are usually a result of internal parts that are worn or rusted, or, more commonly, the seal on the plunger has dried out. These seals are ordinarily made of leather or neoprene and are lubricated with water, oil, graphite, or Vaseline, depending upon the particular model of pump. The lubrication will normally revive the seal, but eventually the seal may have to be replaced if completely worn or dried out.

If a pump fitting is worn or corroded, it will be necessary to disassemble the pump and replace the defective part. Most pumps are easy to take apart—a screwdriver is the only tool needed. Most pump parts are easily available from a local hardware store, while other parts, especially die cast parts, must be ordered from the manufacturer.

The hose of the pump may develop splits after many seasons of hard use. Small tears in the hose can be repaired with a friction tape or silicone rubber sealant. If these repairs fail, the hose can be easily replaced.

ROPE

To lengthen the life of the rope and ensure its strength, the rope should be properly cared for:

- Make sure the rope will not fray or unravel at the ends. Synthetic ropes, easily enough, can be melted with a flame to secure the ends. To prevent natural fiber ropes (such as manila) from unlaying, either wrap the ends with cotton twine or friction tape, or dip the ends in a plastic coating commercially available for that purpose.

- Avoid stepping on the rope. That will damage and shorten its useful life.

- Keep ropes as clean as possible, for dirt that finds its way into the core of the rope will cut the fibers of the rope when tension is applied.

- When not in use, keep ropes coiled neatly and stored in a dry, cool place out of direct sunlight.

- Replace damaged or worn ropes.

Camping Equipment

Despite its durability, camping equipment must be properly cared for to ensure years of hard service. Most camping equipment is simple and functional in design so it can be easily repaired if the need arises.

Clothing. Most campers carry a small sewing kit for the occasional tears in shirts and pants. Nylon fabrics, as used in parkas, sleeping bag shells, and tents, can be repaired temporarily with a ripstop nylon tape that contains adhesive on one side. Permanent repairs in nylon can be patched and sewn with materials in the normal manner. When patching down-filled clothing, use a small diameter needle and fine thread to ensure a down-proof stitch that will prevent the escape of down.

Sleeping bags. After every use, a sleeping bag should be opened up and aired out (preferably outdoors) for a day or two. Spot clean the shell of the sleeping bag with lukewarm, soapy water and sponge with clean water.

If the sleeping bag becomes so soiled it demands more stringent cleaning, it can be washed completely. This cleaning has the effect of redistributing the down that has begun to mat and collect together, leaving large areas in each baffle tube empty.

Both down and synthetic fill sleeping bags can be hand washed. Wash the sleeping bag in a bathtub filled with warm, soapy water—use a mild soap suited for the purpose (especially with down bags). Be especially careful to rinse the bag several times in order to remove all the soap. The bag may be machine washed at a laundromat in a front-loading machine without an agitator but be sure to set the machine on a gentle cycle.

After the bag has been washed and rinsed, remove as much water from the bag as possible. If the bag has been hand washed in a bathtub, gently squeeze water out of the bag. Do not handle a soaked bag, for the increased weight of the down or synthetic fill will tear the internal baffles of the bag. The bag can then be dried outdoors—fluffing the down as it dries out—or in a large commercial tumbler dryer at low heat (with a clean tennis shoe thrown in to break up the clumped down). Never roll up a sleeping bag for storage until it is completely dry. It is best not to store a bag for long periods compressed in a stuff bag. Instead, hang the bag in a closet, roll it loosely, or store it in a large (24 x 30 inch) storage bag made of a breathable fabric.

Down filled sleeping bags can be safely dry cleaned if special care is taken. (Synthetic fills should not be dry cleaned, for the cleaning chemicals may reduce the water repellency and insulating efficiency of the fill.) Down can be damaged by strong dry cleaning solvents, such as chlorinated hydrocarbons, that tend to remove essential oils from the down. Stoddard Fluid, a relatively mild petroleum-based dry cleaning agent, will not have a damaging effect on down products. Especially important is the selection of a dry cleaner who is knowledgeable regarding down. A good outdoor equipment shop should be able to recommend a reliable local cleaning firm. Or ask the dry cleaner about the different cleaning fluids and their effects on down. If you are told it makes no difference or that synthetic fluids such as per-chlorethylene (known in the trade as "perk") are adequate, find a different dry cleaner.

Tents. Unlike canvas, nylon is rot and mildew proof, allowing it to be stored wet for short periods of time. Most nylon tents, however, contain cotton zipper tapes and thread that will rot. When you return home, wash the underside of the tent floor with mild soap to remove dirt particles that can abrade the fabric's waterproof coating. The tent should be erected and completely dried out (and swept out) before final storage.

Occasionally, it is necessary to hand wash nylon tents with a mild soap designed for that purpose and let the tent dry naturally (indoors or out). After drying and before storage, treat the seams of the tent with a waterproofing sealant.

When packing the tent, make sure the points of the tent pegs are protected in a stuff bag to avoid puncturing the tent. Hardware on the tent poses the possibility of abrading the nylon fabric when the tent is rolled up for storage. If possible, pull this hardware to the edges of the roll to protect it from rubbing against the adjacent material. Try not to roll up the tent along the same lines each time—it can weaken the coating along these folds. Tents are best stored in breathable fabric bags to prevent excessive condensation inside the tent.

Stoves. Several precautions will lengthen the life of a camping stove and aid its efficiency. A nylon stuff bag will protect the outside of the stove and keep dirt out of the burner mechanism.

Always keep the gaskets on the pressure pump and fuel tank well lubricated to insure sufficient pressure build-up. (Do not use oil containing solvents which may corrode the gasket.) Always empty the stove before storage because the remaining fuel will form gummy spots that can impair the performance of the stove.

A camping stove is a fairly simple device, so most malfunctions can be remedied with minor adjustments or the replacement of a part or two. If the stove fails to start, it is probably because the pressure in the fuel tank is insufficient. To build up the pressure, make sure the pre-heating is adequate. Fill the burner head with gasoline until it overflows into the priming cup and then reignite.

If the stove starts but will not continue to operate, several possibilities exist. Make sure only white gasoline is used. Automotive gasoline cannot be used for any length of time, as it contans impurities that will clog the burner tip. Avoid any vapor leaks by tightening all parts of the stove. The burner tip may be obstructed, so use the cleaning needle to permit the flow of gas.

Photo courtesy of Maravia Corp.

If there are gas or flame leaks at any point on the stove, try tightening the part, and if the leak still continues, replace the necessary part.

Aluminum cookware. To prevent the warping of aluminum cookware, do not place a hot utensil in cold water or a cold pot over a hot flame. Soaps and cleaners containing strong alkalis such as caustic soda, sal soda, or baking soda should never be used because they will cause pitting.

The discoloration that sometimes occurs on the inside of aluminum cookware is usually due to iron and alkali in the food and water and is perfectly harmless. To remove this discoloration, scour the inside of the pot with a soap-filled scouring pad. Then, dissolve two tablespoons of cream of tartar in each quart of water, and boil this solution in the discolored pot for five to ten minutes. Then scour lightly with a soap-filled scouring pad to restore the original luster of the pot.

Ice chests and beverage coolers. To clean the interior lining of an ice chest or beverage cooler, use a solution of baking soda and water for best results. For odors, wipe the interior lining using a rag saturated with vanilla extract. Leave the rag inside with the lid closed for twenty-four hours to neutralize objectionable odors or tastes.

Epilogue:

Preserving the River Resource

The future of our nation's free-flowing rivers is uncertain, for these rivers have been, and continue to be, subjected to the competing desires of various interest groups. Private companies and governmental agencies both use rivers for the development of water projects, including dam construction, hydroelectric power, municipal water supplies, irrigation, and coal slurrying. Private outdoor recreation does not produce direct monetary revenues, so it is often afforded a lower priority than these economic interests.

One of the greatest threats to free-flowing rivers, and, as a result, to river rafting, has been the construction of dams. Because the planning agency is usually involved in the construction of the project, there is evidence that these agencies are biased in favor of alternatives requiring construction. These agencies have been criticized for failing to consider alternative measures not involving construction, such as the regulation of a flood plain instead of the construction of a dam.

The most common method of evaluating a proposed government project is a cost-benefit analysis, which is, simply stated, an aggregation of all costs and benefits of the proposal. Cost-benefit analysis serves well to justify projects as economically efficient, but problems are encountered when the analysis is used to compare the intangible effects of different projects. Because the benefits derived from outdoor recreation are largely aesthetic, these benefits are often not fully considered.

Even when recreational benefits are considered, these recreational benefits include only the activities that result from the construction of a reservoir. The benefits of free-flowing stream recreation are simply omitted. The recreational benefits of river running must be included to attain a full consideration of the diversified uses of the river.

Despite this disregard for river recreation, a few federal and state statutes provide some optimism for the protection of rivers. A number of general environmental laws require that all environmental impacts of a project must be considered prior to a project's initiation. Water pollution legislation has done a great deal to reduce discharges of toxic pollutants into the nation's waters. A Senate Report expresses the view that "no one has the right to pollute—that pollution continues because of technological limits, not because of any inherent right to use the nation's waterways for disposing of wastes." These new laws left behind the idea of relying upon the assimilative capacity of waterways and made it clear that lakes and streams are no longer part of the waste treatment process.

Another important piece of federal legislation, the Wild and Scenic Rivers Act, affords further protection from development to the rivers classified under the Act. The Act specifies directives for the management of these classified rivers:

> In such administration, primary emphasis shall be given to protecting its esthetic, scenic, historic, archeologic and scientific features.

The Act then classifies rivers as "wild," "scenic," and "recreational" according to the river's degree of development. Each river is, nevertheless, to be managed in order to preserve it as it existed in its free flowing condition.

An important question to resolve is whether the legislative intent of the Act seeks to unconditionally maximize the recreational use of wild rivers. Perhaps recreation should be paramount on those rivers designated as "recreational" under the Act, but in the context of a "wild" river classification, legislative history indicates that the promotion of recreation is not always compatible with the preservation of wilderness aesthetics. A House Report recognizes the potential conflict between recreational use and wilderness aesthetics:

...different streams need to be protected and preserved for different reasons. Some deserve protection solely for their value as completely natural streams. Others deserve protection because of the recreational opportunities they afford. In some instances, these two objectives may be compatible; in others they will be incompatible.

Regardless of the proposed legislation affecting rivers or their recreational use, concerned river runners should express their views and recommendations to congressional members.

Several federal and state agencies are responsible for the administration of many popular rafting rivers. The massive increase in recreational use of these rivers has concerned the managing agencies, and the concept of limiting use by imposing yearly ceilings on use has been implemented. The prevailing view among these agencies is that unless controls are placed on the number of people who are allowed these rivers, then the resource itself may become permanently damaged.

After a ceiling on use has been established, the issue becomes the allocation of this limited resource among the various groups who wish to use it. In the past, agencies have divided the proportions of river use among private and commercial groups. On most rivers the relative percentages were determined by "historical precedent," so that at the time the ceilings were introduced, the relative percentages were set at the level of actual use. This allocation remains fixed, so the system does not account for changes in use that may occur in later years. The central question posed by this system is whether it is a proper exercise of discretion by agencies under the governing statutes and court decisions. Equitable solutions—to both private and commercial groups—are difficult to reach, but the problem requires an examination of the government's duty to the public in the administration of public lands.

These managing agencies nevertheless maintain a great deal of discretion in their administration of river recreation, so river runners must act responsibly to secure the confidence and respect of these agencies. Efficient management of the river resource is necessary to prevent its overuse, and a good rapport between river users and the agency will insure full consideration of the public's suggestions concerning future river regulations.

Most significantly, each individual must take the time and effort to minimize any impacts on the river's environment. The rule of "take nothing but photographs, leave nothing but footprints" is especially important as river running increases in popularity. Special care must be given to trash and human waste disposal, water pollution, and fire prevention.

Decisions concerning the future of our nation's rivers are now being made, but the options, in many cases, are still open. If we fail to preserve these rivers—either through lack of participation in political and administrative processes or through active abuse—we may soon wake up to find that our rivers are lost forever.

Appendix I:

Checklist for Equipment and Gear

Checklists are essential for river trips. Make lists of everything you will need on a particular trip, organizing the equipment and gear according to categories: rafting equipment, kitchen box, personal gear, repair kit and first aid kit.

RAFTING EQUIPMENT

Raft
Frame (and floorboards if used)
Oars (and spares)
Paddles (and spares)
Oarlocks (and oar stoppers with clamps, if used)
Air Pump
Waterproof containers
Life preservers
Rope (including bow and stern lines and rescue line, as well as spare lines)
Nylon webbing straps (for frame tie downs)
First aid kit
Repair kit
Bail bucket (and spare)
Shovel
Channel lock pliers

KITCHEN BOX

Pots and pans
Dutch oven (if used)
Silverware

Long spoon (for stirring)

Can opener

Sierra cups

Collapsible water containers

Fire pan with grill (if fire used)

Camping stove and fuel

Knife

Matches

Newspaper and lighter fluid (if fire used)

Plates

Biodegradable dish soap

Aluminum foil

Paper towels

Plastic bags with fasteners

Pot gripper pliers

Pot scrubber

Water purification (Clorox, Purex, iodine, halazone, or water purifier device)

Salt, pepper, other spices

Sugar (in plastic container)

PERSONAL GEAR

Clothes

    Shirts

    Shorts

    Long pants

    Sweater

    Bandana

    Underwear

    Belt

    Hat

    Gloves

    Down jacket

    Long underwear

    Parka/windbreaker

Shoes

Socks

Swim suit

Dirty clothes sack

Sleeping and Shelter

Sleeping bag

Foam pad/air mattress

Bivouac cover

Tent (with poles, pegs)

Tarp

Other

Flashlight (with spare batteries and bulb)

Biodegradable hand soap

Sunglasses

Suntan lotion

Lip balm

Towel

Toothbrush, toothpaste

Toilet paper

Mosquito repellent

Nylon line

Needles and thread

Camera

Fishing gear

Binoculars

Knife

REPAIR KIT

Raft patching material (1 square yard)

Adhesive (1 quart)

Solvent/thinner (1 quart)

Small brush (for applying glue)

Buffer tool/sandpaper (for roughing area to be patched)

Rolling tool (for pressing down patches)

Pair of scissors

Upholstery needles (for sewing larger tears)

Nylon or waxed thread

Duct tape

Epoxy glue

Silicone rubber sealant/troweling compound

Bailing wire

Spare parts (vary according to type of raft and frame used, but include such items as assorted nuts and bolts, valves, "D" rings, and radiator hose clips)

FIRST AID KIT

Items to be included in a first aid kit for river use are included on page 115 of chapter 6. These items should be kept clean, dry, and in good repair at all times. Before each trip, check the first aid kit to make sure all items used on a previous trip have been replaced, and that all medications are fresh.

Appendix II:

Sources of Rafts and Equipment

The following list of companies includes the manufacturers and importers of river rafts. In addition to their line of rafts, most of these companies also stock air pumps, "D" rings, and repair materials. Some also sell frames and waterproof bags. A few, most notably Campways and Northwest River Supplies, carry a wide range of related rafting equipment including paddles, oars, oarlocks, webbing straps, lifejackets, ice chests, and coolers. The camping equipment necessary for river trips is widely available from outdoor equipment catalogs and shops throughout the country.

Avon
Seagull Marine
1851 McGaw Avenue
Irvine, California 92714

Campways
12915 South Spring Street
Los Angeles, California 90061

Maravia Corporation
Box 395
San Leandro, California 94577

Mountain State Inflatables
Box 265
Fenwick, West Virginia 26202

Northwest River Supplies
Box 9243
Moscow, Idaho 83843

Rafts West
512 E. Leland Avenue
Salt Lake City, Utah 84106

Rogue Inflatables
8500 Galice Road
Merlin, Oregon 97532

Rubber Crafters of West Virginia
Box 220
Grantsville, West Virginia 26147

UDISCO
Box 15658
Salt Lake City, Utah 84115

World Famous, Inc.
3580 N. Elston Avenue
Chicago, Illinois 60618

Zodiac of North America, Inc.
11 Lee Street
Annapolis, Maryland 21401

Appendix III:

Where to Write
for River Information
and Permits

One of the most important tasks in preparing for a river trip is the collection of information relating to the river. This information, for example, will list the times of the year and the river levels and flows most suitable for rafting. The possible lengths of trips, as well as put-in and take-out points, are shown. River permits are increasingly required as a prerequisite to running the river. These permits, designed to reduce the environmental impact on the river, must often be secured months in advance—*write early.* Most importantly, this river information is necessary from a safety aspect, for it reveals the level of difficulty and hazards of the river.

Federal

Most of the popular rafting rivers in the country flow through federal lands and are administered by one of the federal agencies. The great majority of these rivers are managed by the U.S. Department of Agriculture through the Forest Service or by the U.S. Department of the Interior through either the National Park Service or the Bureau of Land Management. Included are the addresses of the regional offices of these agencies, as well as a list of specific rivers and their managing agencies, grouped according to the state where the river is located.

U. S. Forest Service
Department of Agriculture
Washington, D.C. 20250

Northern Region, Federal Building, Missoula, Montana 59801

Southwestern Region, 517 Gold Avenue, S.W., Albuquerque, New Mexico 87102

California Region, 630 Sansome Street, San Francisco, California 94111

Intermountain Region, 324 25th Street, Ogden, Utah 84401

Pacific Northwest Region, 319 Southwest Pine Street, P.O. Box 3623, Portland, Oregon 97208

Eastern Region, 633 West Wisconsin Avenue, Milwaukee, Wisconsin 53203

Southern Region, 1720 Peachtree Road, N.W., Atlanta, Georgia 30309

Alaska Region, Federal Office Building, P.O. Box 1628, Juneau, Alaska 99502

National Park Service
Department of Interior
Washington, D.C. 20240

Northeast Region, 143 South Third Street, Philadelphia, Pennsylvania 19106

Southwest Region, P.O. Box 728, Santa Fe, New Mexico 87501

Western Region, 450 Golden Gate Avenue, Box 36036, San Francisco, California 94102

Midwest Region, 1709 Jackson Street, Omaha, Nebraska 68102

Southeast Region, 3401 Whipple Avenue, Atlanta, Georgia 30344

Bureau of Land Management
Department of Interior
Washington, D.C. 20240

Alaska State Office, 555 Cordova Street, Anchorage, Alaska 99510

Arizona State Office, 2400 Bank Center, Phoenix, Arizona 85073

California State Office, Federal Building, 2800 Cottage Way, Sacramento, California 95825

Colorado State Office, Room 700, Colorado State Bank Building, 1600 Broadway, Denver, Colorado 80202

Eastern States Office, 7981 Eastern Avenue, Silver Springs, Maryland 20910

Montana State Office, Granite Tower, 222 No. 32nd Street, P.O. Box 30157, Billings, Montana 30157

Nevada State Office, Federal Building, 300 Booth Street, Reno, Nevada 89509

New Mexico State Office, Federal Building, South Federal Place, Santa Fe, New Mexico 87501

Oregon State Office, 729 N.E. Oregon Street, P.O. Box 2965, Portland, Oregon 97208

Utah State Office, University Club Building, 136 East South Temple, Salt Lake City, Utah 84111

Wyoming State Office, 2515 Warren Avenue, Cheyenne, Wyoming 82001

ALASKA

Anchorage Dist. Office
555 Cordova Street
Anchorage, Alaska 99501

Various Alaskan rivers

Glennallen Resource Area
Box 147
Glennallen, Alaska 99588

Delta,
Gulkana

ARIZONA

Glen Canyon NRA
P.O. Box 1507
Page, Arizona 86040

Colorado (Glen Canyon Dam to Lee's Ferry), San Juan (below Mexican Hat)

Grand Canyon Nat'l Park
P.O. Box 129
Grand Canyon, Arizona 86023

Colorado (within park

Havasu Resource Area
P.O. Box 685
Lake Havasu, Arizona 86403

Lower Colorado (Parker to Davis)

Yuma Resource Area
2450 4th Avenue
Yuma, Arizona 85364

Lower Colorado (Border to Parker)

ARKANSAS

Buffalo National River
P.O. Box 1173
Harrison, Arkansas 72601

Buffalo

CALIFORNIA

Folsom Dist. Office
63 Natoma Street
Folsom, California 95630

Stanislaus-American (North-South & Mid-Forks), Consumnes, Mokelumne, Merced, Yuba

Klamath Nat'l Forest
1215 S. Main
Yreka, Calif. 96097

Klamath,
Salmon,
Scott

Plumas Nat'l Forest 159 Lawrence Avenue Quincy, Calif. 95971	Feather River-Middle Fork
Sequoia Nat'l Forest 800 Truxtun Avenue Bakersfield, Calif. 93301	Kern
Shasta-Trinity Nat'l Forest 1615 Continental Street Redding, Calif. 96001	Sacramento, Trinity, Canyon Creek, Hayfork Creek
Sierra Nat'l Forest P.O. Box 747 Mariposa, Calif. 95338	Merced
Sierra Nat'l Forest Timmer Route Sanger, Calif. 93657	Kings River
Six Rivers Nat'l Forest 710 E Street Eureka, Calif. 95501	Smith, Mad, Eel
Stanislaus Nat'l Forest Box 90 Groveland, Calif. 95321	Tuolumne
Tahoe Nat'l Forest Nevada City, Calif. 95959	American-North Fork

COLORADO

Dinosaur Nat'l Monument P.O. Box 210 Dinosaur, Colo. 86040	Green (within Monument), Yampa (within Monument)
Glenwood Springs Res. Area Box 1009 Glenwood Springs, Colo. 81601	Colorado (Upper), Eagle
Routt Nat'l Forest Walden, Colo. 80480	North Platte (North Gate Canyon)

IDAHO

Boise Dist. Office 230 Collins Road Boise, Idaho 83702	Owhee (above Three Forks), Bruneau Jarbridge
Challis Nat'l Forest Challis, Idaho 83226	Middle Fork of the Salmon
Clearwater Nat'l Forest Kooskia, Idaho 83539	Lochsa, Clearwater-Middle Fork

Cottonwood Resource Area
Route 3
Cottonwood, Idaho 83522

Salmon (French Cr.-Snake River),
Snake (Zig-Zag Cr.-Cougar Bar on
the Idaho side)

Idaho Panhandle Nat'l Forest
Sandpoint, Idaho 83864

Prest, St. Joe

Nez Perce Nat'l Forest
Kooskia, Idaho 83539

Selway, Clearwater-Middle Fork

Nez Perce Nat'l Forest
White Bird, Idaho 83554

Salmon (N. Fork to Riggins),
Snake (Hell's Canyon)

Payette Nat'l Forest
Council, Idaho 83612

Snake (Hell's Canyon)

Salmon Nat'l Forest
North Fork, Idaho 83466

Salmon (Salmon River Canyon)

Sawtooth NRA
Stanley, Idaho 83278

Salmon (upper)

Targhee Nat'l Forest
Island Park, Idaho

Snake-Henry's Fork

Targhee Nat'l Forest
Rexburg, Idaho 83440

Snake-South Fork (Grand Canyon),
Snake (Palisades-Heise)

MISSOURI

Ozark Nat'l Scenic Riverways
Van Buren, Mo. 62965

Current, Jacks Fork

MONTANA

Bitterroot Nat'l Forest
Darby, Mont. 59829

Selway

Flathead Nat'l Forest
Kalispell, Mont. 59901

3-Forks Flathead River

NEVADA

Carson City Dist. Office
801 N. Plaza
Carson City, Nev. 89701

Carson-East Fork

Lake Mead NRA
601 Nevada Highway
Boulder City, Nev. 89005

Colorado (Within NRA)

Toiyabe Nat'l Forest
1536 S. Carson
Carson City, Nev. 89701

East Carson

OREGON

Prineville District 185 East 4th Street Prineville, Ore. 97753	John Day Deschutes
Medford District 310 W. Sixth South Medford, Ore. 97501	Rogue
Siskiyou Nat'l Forest Box 440 Grants Pass, Ore. 97526	Illinois
Vale District Box 700 Vale, Ore. 97918	Owyhee (Three Forks) to Owyhee (Reservoir)
Wallowa-Whitman Nat'l Forest Federal Office Building Box 907 Baker, Ore. 97814	Grande Ronde, Snake (Hell's Canyon)

SOUTH CAROLINA

Sumter Nat'l Forest Star Route Walhalla, S.C. 29691	Chattooga

TEXAS

Big Bend Nat'l Park Big Bend NP, Tex. 79834	Rio Grande (within park)

UTAH

Canyonlands Nat'l Park 446 South Main Moab, Utah 84532	Colorado (within park) Green (within park)
Grand Resource Area 446 South Main Moab, Utah 84532	Colorado (Westwater Canyon), Colorado (Rose Ranch to Castle Cr.), Dolores (Utah part)
Flaming Gorge NRA Dutch John, Utah 84032	Green (below dam)
North Vernal Resource Area P.O. Box F Vernal, Utah 84078	Green (Little Hole to Brown's Park)
Price Resource Area P.O. Drawer AB Price, Utah 84501	Green (Desolation-Gray Canyon)

San Juan Resource Area
P.O. Box 1327
Monticello, Utah 84532

San Juan (above Mexican Hat)

WYOMING

Brigder-Teton Nat'l Forest
Afton, Wyo. 83110

Greys

Grand Teton Nat'l Park
P.O. Box 67
Moose, Wyo. 83012

Snake (within park)

State

Several rivers not located on federal lands are administered by state agencies, while other rivers cross privately owned lands. Sources of information concerning these rivers are scattered, but information can usually be obtained from state agencies. Since several state agencies may provide information relating to a particular river, it is advisable to write all of the appropriate agencies to obtain as much information as possible. Write the following agencies at the state capitol:

- State Parks and Recreation
- State Department of Natural Resources and Conservation
- State Department of Commerce and Tourism
- State Fish and Game Commission

Other Sources

Guide books and annotated maps of rivers provide useful information relating to access points, favorable rafting season, river difficulty and specific river hazards. These guide books are available in most outdoor equipment catalogs and stores, and a complete list of books of interest to river runners is stocked by Westwater Books, P.O. Box 365, Boulder City, Nevada 89005. Still other sources of information exist. The local chamber of commerce or police department may be able to provide information concerning current river conditions. Commercial outfitters in the area are also helpful in offering relevant information.

About the Author

Cecil Kuhne began rafting during his college years and has spent numerous summers as a professional river guide. He has led trips on the Colorado River through Cararact Canyon and Grand Canyon and on the Rio Grande in Big Bend National Park. He is also a Contributing Editor to *River World* magazine specializing in articles on rafting and river camping. When Cecil is not rafting or working as a guide, he is a practicing attorney, concentrating on natural resources law.

Kuhne, a resident of Lubbock, Texas, is a graduate of Texas Tech University and Texas Christian University.

River Rafting is his first book.

Acknowledgments

This book would not have been possible without the help of many people. I would like to thank publisher Bob Anderson for his direction of the project. I am also grateful to *River World* editor Pam Miller for her encouragement that kept me writing articles for the magazine while I was preparing the manuscript. And thanks to Lynne Steele for her fine copy editing work.

I appreciate the assistance of Richard Ford, President of Maravia Corporation, for his assistance with the sections of the book dealing with raft design and the newer materials used in raft construction. Earl Huffman, President of Mountain State Inflatables, was extremely helpful in providing information regarding the manufacture of rafts.

I would especially like to thank the many river guides and acquaintances I have met on the river, all of whom have sparked and sustained my enthusiasm for rafting. I extend special thanks to my personal friends and fellow river rafters Roger Elam, Kelly Pratas, Mike Bryam, Gene Vinzant, and Ray Bryant for their encouragement of the project. I am also greatly indebted to Cherie Grant for her tireless work with the illustrations and the typing of the manuscript.

Recommended Reading

Rocky Mountain National Park Trail Guide by Erik Nilsson. Answers all questions about this beautiful park. There is clear, detailed information on equipment, safety, and camping regulations, along with charts and topographical maps, to help all campers. Paperback, $3.95

Scuba Diving Safety by Christopher W. Dueker, M. D. The challenges of diving arise because it is a vigorous sport undertaken in a potentially hostile environment. This is what makes the authoritative information in *Scuba Diving Safety* so valuable. Paperback, $3.95.

Basic Swimming Guide by Joseph K. Groscost. The *Basic Swimming Guide* has plenty of practical advice on teaching children how to swim. It deals with common problems in learning swimming strokes, and offers proven and practical solutions. Paperback, $2.50

The Backpacker's Guide by W.R.C. Shedenhelm. All the information needed for planning backpacking trips—for a day or for a week—is included. There is information on proper equipment along with cures for common ailments. Paperback, $4.95

3,000 Miles By Canoe by Dale Witmer. Follow the Witmers on their thrilling canoe journey down the Missouri and Mississippi rivers. Witmer gives the canoeist sound advice based on the wide range of problems he had to face and overcome. Paperback, $4.95

River World Magazine. *River World* is one of the top publications for canoeists, kayakers, and rafters. There is comprehensive coverage of news in the fields of touring and competition, how-to advice for novice and expert alike, equipment reviews, more. (Seven issues, April-October), $6.50

Available in fine bookstores and sport shops, or from:

World Publications, Inc.

Box 366, Mountain View, CA 94042

Include $.45 shipping and handling for each title (Maximum $2.25).